THE INTERIORS BOOK OF
SHOPS & RESTAURANTS

THE INTERIORS BOOK OF
SHOPS & RESTAURANTS

By the Editors of INTERIORS Magazine

With Commentaries by
Pilar Viladas

WHITNEY LIBRARY OF DESIGN
an imprint of Watson-Guptill Publications/New York

The Architectural Press Ltd./London

First published 1981 in the United States and Canada by Whitney Library of Design,
an imprint of Watson-Guptill Publications,
a division of Billboard Publications, Inc.,
1515 Broadway, New York, N.Y. 10036

Library of Congress Cataloging in Publication Data
Main entry under title:
The Interiors book of shops & restaurants.
    Includes index.
    1. Interior decoration—United States—History—
20th century. 2. Store decoration—United States.
3. Restaurants, lunch rooms, etc.—United States—
Decoration. 4. Showrooms—United States—Decoration.
5. Shopping malls—United States—Decoration. 6. Market-
places—United States—Decoration. I. Interiors.
NK2004.I57   725'.21'0973   81-65
ISBN 0-8230-7284-3

Published in Great Britain by The Architectural Press Ltd.,
9 Queen Anne's Gate, London SW1H 9BY
ISBN 0-85139-327-6

Manufactured in Japan

First Printing, 1981

CONTENTS

Introduction, 6

SHOPS & STORES, 7

I. Magnin, 8
Bullock's, Newport Beach, California, 10
Botticelli Shop, 14
Vidal Sassoon, 16
Abitare, 18
Conran's, New York, 22
Conran's, New Rochelle, New York, 26
Charrette, 28
AT&T, 30
80 West 40th Street, New York, 34
Hall's Plaza, 38
Bullock's, San Jose, California, 42
1610 Chestnut Street, Philadelphia, 44
Courrèges Boutique, 50
The Arrangement, 52
Janice Julian, 54
Julio, 56
Schullin, 58
Bulgari Jewellers Danaos Ltd., 62

RESTAURANTS, 65

Arby's, 66
Les Ombrages, 68
Sacco Caffé, 72
Confetti Café, 73
Healthworks, 74
U.S. Steakhouse Company, 76
The Katonah Railroad Station, 80

Paramount Commissary, 82
The Basement, 86
Greens, 88
The Sandwich Construction Company, 90
Café Fanny, 92
Le Premier, 96
One Fifth, 100
Gordana's, 102

SHOWROOMS, 105

Knoll International, 106
MIRA-X, 107
Professional Kitchen, 108
Brickel Associates Inc./Ward Bennett Designs, 109
Andrew Geller, 110
Steelcase, 112
Eurotex, 114
The Pace Collection, 115
Sunar, 116
Erbun Fabrics, 118
Thonet, 120

MALLS & MARKETPLACES, 125

Hulen Mall, 126
Mayfair in the Grove, 130
Citicorp Center, 134
World Trade Center, 138

Illustration Credits, 144

Index of Designers, 144

INTRODUCTION

The decade of the seventies launched a whole new approach to merchandising services, spurred by the revolutionary events of the sixties. The flower children of the Beatle Generation were finally heard and catered to—with health food restaurants, unisex hair stylists, warehouse clothes emporiums, no frills supermarkets, and ethnic bazaars. Interior design reflected the beat of the new-think customer, concerned with back-to-nature pursuits, resource recycling, ecological consciousness-raising—all with a liberal lacing of soul, rock, or folk rhythms.

The exposed-brick-and-fern school of design became an accepted style for shops, stores, restaurants, and malls as more and more retailers thrived in renovated factories, wharves, and other until recently unused industrial spaces. This was the quick and obvious way to go. Other more thoughtful designers mirrored the changing public tastes in subtler ways—creating stylistic indoor/outdoor fantasies, introducing nostalgia, meeting the electronic sound wave head on with extraordinary lighting effects, playing hi-tech against low-tech, the ultimate response to the crisscrossed, nature-with-computer-assist, bargain-hunting public. If there is one overall observation to be made, it is that there is no single design idiom which characterizes the seventies selling techniques. Indeed, what makes the era distinctive is its pluralism. In fact, the respect for quality handwork and natural materials seems to indicate that the legacy from the decade is a renewed interest in craftsmanship and decoration. While this may be a reaction to cheap, machine-made, mass-produced imitation and an excessive infatuation with plastics, there is a new appreciation for stained and etched glass, ceramics, fine wood carving, wrought iron, lacquering, hand painting. In the heyday of modernist design vocabulary, such artisan work was dismissed as irrelevant. Today it is respected as enrichment to interiors.

If radical individualism was the cult of the sixties, interior design caught up with it in the seventies. The eighties indicate increasing liberation in design to meet the demand for retailing alternatives.

Beverly Russell, Editor-in-Chief, *Interiors* Magazine

SHOPS & STORES

The past decade has seen astonishing growth in retail design. The rise of the boutique and the shopping mall has helped to change the face of the American retail landscape from one populated largely by department stores and small specialty shops to one offering the shopper a staggering variety of choices. And this is precisely the point. By the end of the 1970s, more than 70 percent of the merchandise in a large department store was identical with that in any other large department store. Presentation, therefore, has become a crucial factor, and the key to presentation is design. Consumers are growing increasingly sophisticated and increasingly concerned with individualism. They don't want to feel like numbers in the cash register; they want to feel special. Consequently, there is now a growing demand for novelty, which in turn fosters greater diversity and creativity in design.

Several factors within our culture have influenced current trends in retail design. The rise of consumerism, coupled with the emphasis on individualism that finds extreme expression in the narcissism of the "Me Generation," has gone hand in hand with an unprecedented rise in consumer spending, despite the fact that the seventies were a decade of economic uncertainty. Obviously, people are spending money, whether they can afford to or not, and they want to enjoy themselves at the same time.

In the general rush to make shopping a more enticing and eventful experience, eclecticism is the watchword of retail design. Several major design trends seem to have evolved in the process, each of them catering to a specific shopping and merchandising philosophy. The most prevalent and probably the most enduring of these is the modern or mainstream approach. Its classic look is one that is popular in department stores, such as I. Magnin or Bullock's, shown on the following pages; but it can be applied with equal success in a small space, such as the Botticelli shoe store or the Vidal Sassoon hair salon. It is clean; color schemes are generally low-key; materials are often simple but luxurious. The look can range from a sort of high-tech chic, as in the Sassoon salon, to European luxe, as in Bullock's Newport Beach. The point is to create a pleasant, soothing environment to make the shopper feel pampered; these spaces are intended to boost the consumer's ego in a subtle way, to make him feel as if he has come to exactly the right place. When applied in a department store setting, this type of design, which is often reliant upon architectural elements for its drama, provides a conservative backdrop for merchandise, one that is acceptable to a broad cross section of

the buying public. When applied in a small boutique setting, however, it is versatile enough to be seen as ultrafashionable understatement—an affirmation of the customer's low-key good taste.

At the other end of the scale is the design philosophy that can be characterized as no-frills. A product of the recently blossomed consumer movement, the no-frills approach is based on a time-honored principle: that is, that almost anything costs less without the trimmings. It has worked with great success for many years in factory outlets and discount stores, where volume buying, and not decor, is the investment priority. The ambience may not be much, and neither are the amenities, but the prices are right. Retail designers have successfully investigated this "warehouse" approach to merchandising, especially during the past few years, when minimalism in interior design became an important force in the industry; the time was ripe to try it out in the consumer marketplace. The merchandise is allowed to speak for itself in a deliberately uncluttered environment. Whether in a high-priced, high-design setting like Abitare, or a moderately priced, mass-appeal store like Conran's, the message is the same: "No gimmicks here." The customer feels that he sees exactly what he is getting, minus any merchandising tricks. Of course, the design philosophy itself is the merchandising strategy, but when aimed at the right market, it can be extremely successful. It is also perfectly appropriate to the more "technical" purposes of stores such as Charrette, which sells architectural supplies, or the AT&T telephone store, where the latest in telephone design is offered to the consumer. In both cases, the no-nonsense feeling is well conveyed.

Another offshoot of the 1960s and 1970s is a design philosophy that can be called "historical recall." It goes hand in hand with the dramatic increase in popularity of adaptive reuse of older buildings, as well as with our growing appreciation of our architectural past and natural materials. More and more older buildings are being rehabilitated for retail use, and architects and designers are taking great care to let the best qualities of the past speak for themselves. What this means in terms of design is that columns and moldings are left intact or restored, wood floors are refinished, and lots of natural materials are used. Large windows, a luxury of bygone days, provide welcome natural light (an energy-saving plus) and often foster the presence of veritable jungles of green plants. This style works with equal ease in a building that dates from the turn of the century, such as the project at 80 West 40th Street in New York,

or on a relatively new building, such as Hall's Plaza in Kansas City or Bullock's San Jose, in which a modern design vocabulary is combined with natural materials to create a sunny, relaxed feeling—an informal, friendly atmosphere in which to shop. This type of retail design has met with enormous success in urban "mini-mall" projects, where its informality, repeated in several different shops, creates a festive, bazaarlike atmosphere. And its basic neutrality makes it the perfect backdrop for everything from general department store merchandise (Hall's and Bullock's) to designer fashions (80 West 40th Street) to sophisticated home furnishings and fabrics (1610 Chestnut Street in Philadelphia).

Quite apart from the simplicity of natural and no-frills design is the most recent and perhaps most interesting of the trends in retail design, one that can be called "shopping as theater." Perhaps a product, more than anything else, of the narcissistic seventies, this approach focuses squarely on making the consumer the center of the action, the key participant in the exciting experience of shopping. It turns the simple act of choosing and paying for a simple item into a flight of fantasy. The elements of drama and surprise are crucial; the shopper wants to be amused and excited—and never, ever bored. Using everything from shocking window displays to videotaped fashion shows to fantastic architectural designs, the consumer is made to feel the center of attention, as in the Courrèges Boutique, which is essentially a slick, futuristic stage set. This approach is especially valid in beauty salons, whether it is carried out in a simple, witty design vocabulary (The Arrangement), a high-tech, pop-star mode (Janice Julian), or a fanciful exercise in handcraftsmanship of ornate decor (Julio). It is also well suited to the two jewelry stores shown here (Schullin and Bulgari Danaos), in which the architects have exploited the theme of the guarded bank vault to create an atmosphere of mystery (with a hint of danger), luxury, and—above all, in view of the high cost of the merchandise—exclusivity. When you are shelling out $50,000 for a ring, that inner-sanctum feeling is essential. The retail store as theater is perhaps the ultimate in ego-gratification for the consumer.

The categories outlined here are by no means inflexible; part of the excitement in retail design today is its ever-changing nature. Furthermore, it is clear that the possibilities of merchandising by design are just starting to be explored. The important thing is that retailers everywhere have begun to realize that design is crucial for moving their goods out of the store.

I. MAGNIN

The location may be Maryland, but the feeling is California. That is precisely the impression that I. Magnin wanted to create in its first East Coast store, located at White Flint, a fashionable shopping mall in Bethesda. Designers Copeland, Novak & Israel of New York emphasized variety and theatricality through an interplay of space, architectural forms, and rich colors and materials. The stylistic components had to be sophisticated yet simple, in keeping with Magnin's high-fashion image.

Several "givens" faced the designers, the most challenging of which was the pre-fixed location of the escalators. This was turned into an architectural and merchandising asset by the creation of an octagonal escalator well made of transparent glass, which serves as both a dramatic merchandise showcase and a focal point for each of the two floors.

The architectural design stresses shop definition while still allowing for visual penetration for a feeling of spatial, as well as merchandising, variety. Structural elements define and enclose individual shops, and multilevel ceiling planes are placed in counterpoint to the shapes of the departments and circulation systems. These elements not only enclose space, but frame it theatrically in the manner of proscenium arches.

The luxurious, sunny-California mood is the result of a careful orchestration of colors, textures, and materials. Travertine aisles, bronze-tinted glass, and burled, bleached-wood veneers strike elegant notes, while raw silks, straw, and handwoven cottons evoke a natural spirit. The designers used incandescent lighting wherever possible to reinforce the warm feeling, and the West Coast aura is further intensified by an extravagent use of plantings. The striking architectural forms, sophisticated spatial organization, and rich materials combine to create an effect of casual elegance and understated luxury.

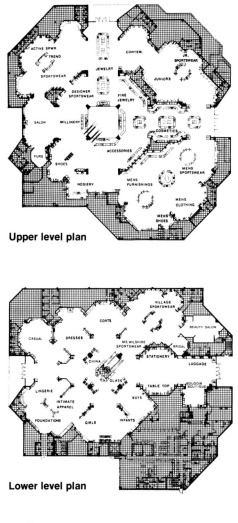

Upper level plan

Lower level plan

Floor plans (above) reflect angularity of building design by Welton Becket Associates. Central glass-walled escalators (right) are angled also and rise toward a mirrored octagonal column and a ceiling subtly painted in Art Deco patterns. Here and throughout the store, planting is generous.

BULLOCK'S,
NEWPORT BEACH, CALIFORNIA

When the original Bullock's Wilshire opened on Los Angeles's Wilshire Boulevard in 1928, it was an exuberant—in fact, a quite stupefying—triumph of Art Deco stylization. It still is. The design, by Donald and John Parkinson, was exemplary not only in its decoration, but also in its planning: although the general building massing paid lip service to Wilshire Boulevard, the main entrance—with ceiling fresco and uniformed doorman—was quite definitely and logically at the rear, facing the parking lot. The store was also one of the most elegant in the country, built for an affluent clientele on the merry eve of the Depression.

When the Woodland Hills branch was added some years later, the Art Deco theme was repeated, and Bullock's over the years has capitalized on the same image in its interior displays and in its advertising. When Copland, Novak & Israel were asked to design the store's branch in Newport Beach, California, therefore, the precedent of Art Deco allusion was already established. Also established—by Bullock's own store-planning unit—were adjacency, layerage, and departmental allocation diagrams. Further requirements were that the store must attract the "carriage trade" without seeming forbidding to young suburbanites, that it must reflect not only the store's tradition but also the casual resort atmosphere of its location, and that, of course, it must be complementary to the existing two-level shopping mall and to the building shell designed by architects Welton Becket and Associates.

The Becket firm had given the store a distinctive envelope seemingly based on a complex grouping of octagonal elements. Without slavishly following the building outline, the interior design clearly repeats and capitalizes on its angular character. As Copeland, Novak & Israel partner Adolph Novak has written in his recent and useful book, *Store Planning and Design*, "There are stores that operate very successfully within odd shapes, using apses and other restricted areas to locate limited categories of merchandise. This can present a boutique appearance [and provides] a more exciting store design than the usual box-shaped square or rectangle."

The plan is further elaborated by means of distinct aisle systems on both levels. On the upper level, an aisle of warm brown square quarry tile connects the central escalator well with a door to a parking field and another to the upper level of the open mall. On the lower level, aisles of rust-colored geometric-patterned carpet connect the central well to two other entrances, one to an enclosed parking deck, the other to the lower mall level. The location of the glass-walled escalators (the first escalators to be used in a Bullock's store) is central, but the escalators have been turned 45° to the building's main axes, further adding to the dynamic quality of the interior.

Colors throughout are low-keyed and muted, with taupes, browns, and naturals predominating; lighting, too, is low, in accordance both with the interior's desired character and with new California criteria for reduced energy consumption (criteria not yet in effect as the store was being designed, but followed nevertheless). Primary light sources are recessed incandescents, supplemented by fluorescents at the cornice line and strong accent spotlights.

The end result: an interior of subtlety, style, and—to use a word from the Art Deco era—swank.

(Left and opposite page, top middle) Details of the store's central escalator well. Mirrored columns at the corners of the space repeat the octagonal motif and also gently recall the Art Deco character of the original store in the chain. On display cases, upper floor fascia, and escalator parapet is beige suede vinyl. (Opposite page, top left) Opening directly from the central circulation area (carpeted in a geometric figure of chamois and rust) is a gift and china boutique. Display units are visually recessive—mirrored, clear, or plain white. Display niches with flexible shelving are topped with panels of ginger suede; behind the panels is accent lighting. (Opposite page, below) Shoe salon on the upper floor uses a deep version of the store's predominant color scheme of brown and taupe; low lighting level adds glamour and saves watts. Octagonal mirrored drums repeat the basic geometry of the store's exterior. Cream lacquer chairs at the rear of the salon have light taupe upholstery. Upholstered loveseat is behind mirrored column.

botticelli

BOTTICELLI SHOP

Construction *will* hit snarls, and a small space can complicate planning. In the design of the Botticelli shoe and luggage shop at Rockefeller Plaza in Manhattan the I-beam (painted red) had to be delivered at 4:00 A.M. and immediately fitted into its diagonal position, as "there was nowhere to lay it down," say the designers of Stedila Design, Inc. They enlarged the former Delta Airlines ticket office by creating vertical and horizontal space where all levels of activity are visible. A steel grille forms an exposed second level with a spiral staircase leading to storage (which becomes part of the design with white shoe boxes—3,000 of them—on metal shelving against matte black walls). Stepped-up carpeted platforms are used for seating and display. Other elements that visually enlarge the space and give a sense of turning corners are the mirror-panel baffles running up into the grille and indirect lighting behind the panels and under the banquettes. Silvery track fixtures and the neon sculpture add a bit of theater and whimsy. Seating upholstery is trough-quilted in a brushed, suedelike cotton dress fabric.

John Stedila founded his firm in 1972 and soon added contract work to residential design through commissions from the Seventh Avenue fashion world. Since Tim Button joined the firm three years later, the work has broadened to encompass banks, offices, and a discotheque.

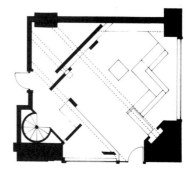

VIDAL SASSOON

In a remarkable film sequence by the Office of Charles and Ray Eames, a young man at the circus transforms his distinctly handsome physiognomy into the face of a classic clown. We watch and listen with him as he paces himself against the musical cues that mark circus time. The process is fascinating—a young man's countenance disappears behind the universal face of the clown. It is the same concern for the transition from private to public face that animates the Vidal Sassoon salon in Water Tower Place in Chicago by Gwathmey-Siegel, architects.

Sassoon is a noted hair stylist whose distinctive cuts, consistent craftsmanship, and invitation to clients and apprentices to observe the entire process have established him firmly in the fashion field. As a major designer of his salons, Gwathmey-Siegel has been charged with interpreting his style in architectonic terms. Sassoon salons, varying from 3,500 to 5,000 sq ft (325 to 464½ m²) in size, consequently reflect a strong sense of order, sequence—and psychology, too.

There are fifty work stations for one hundred staff members and their clients on 4,500 sq ft (418 m²) in Chicago. Keeping so many people and activities under control requires precise circulation paths, so the designer bends the movement into tight, B-shaped closed loops. A typical client sequence: register at appointment desk, check coat, don robe in dressing room, take seat or proceed to hair wash, take seat at cutting station (stopping for hair drying if needed), and reverse sequence. Although the two-thirds of the total space occupied by women is more open than the men's, the programs are identical.

Gwathmey-Siegel's design is formal, spare, yet surprisingly ethereal. Its most colorful accessories are the clients themselves, shown to their advantage against clean white fascia; task lighting from track-mounted down cans with ambient globe diffusers; neutral tones in casework, seating, and floor tiles; and a variety of surfaces that alter light. Light is the principal form giver here. Broad sheets of mirror make a *tableau vivant* of the cutting rooms; aluminum ceiling pans extend elevation lines to infinity; and glass-block walls shimmer with the commotion of the public life waiting outside.

The total effect is like a voyage through space—even the sleek registration desk with its display cases of Sassoon products resembles a ship's bridge. And why not? As Charles Gwathmey says, "This is meant to be a surreal environment. You come for more than a haircut. You come for the trip."

Space above appointment desk (left) seems infinite because of reflective ceiling at Sassoon. Other ambiguities appear in view from public corridor inside (below), cutting stations (opposite page, top), and washing sinks (opposite page, bottom).

Steel truss spans new facade at second floor, allowing the elimination of first floor columns. White stripes on glass spell out "Abitare" (with graphics by Marjorie Katz Design).

At top of stair (above) a glass-walled conference room. Below the stair (above right) a wrap desk and, beyond it, a display of lighting by Antonio Morello and Donato Savoie of Morsa.

ABITARE

"Come alone, bring a friend, your architect, or your decorator," says an eight-page brochure. This unusually flexible invitation is for shopping at Abitare, which means "living" in Italian and which calls itself "New York's most exciting new furniture store."

The store is owned by Techinteriors, a savvy group headed by Jim Mauri, formerly with Knoll International for fourteen years and also founder of a consulting firm, Marketing Design Associates. Vice-president of Techinteriors is Margarita Cahn, previously with Robert S. McMillan Associates, architects and planners. The store has a savvy location, too: the former home of the Meredith Galleries on East 57th Street, among Manhattan's greatest concentration of fine shops and design showrooms. It has been the subject of much conversation—not all of it admiring—in those same showrooms, for Abitare, as its invitation suggests, has ignored the to-the-trade-only policy that has become traditional for selling "designer" furniture (in Abitare's case, mostly Italian imports) in the

United States. The store does cooperate with design professionals, however; it does give a *small* discount on occasion; and it is making plans for distributing catalogs to design firms. And some of the furniture it sells without benefit of exclusivity—Mies and Breuer chairs, for example (Abitare calls them "reproductions" rather than "copies")—is very competitively priced.

In the store's design, too, tradition has been ignored. The interior designer was Robin Jacobsen, who has done, among other fine work, some excellent showroom design for Knoll; the architect was Scott Bromley. The result of the Jacobsen-Bromley collaboration is very unlike either today's typical well-designed store or today's typical well-designed showroom. There are no boutiquelike cubicles, no partitions, no platforms—no spatial divisions at all except those created by dramatic pools of light. On the other hand, despite the general openness, there is none of the look of a big furniture warehouse, no sea of sofas or parade of end tables. This is an in-

terior with quite an imaginative, individual personality. It may be spare, but there is nothing spartan about it.

One major determinant of the design was the response by Jacobsen and Bromley to the existing building shell. Except for the facade, which they stripped away, boldly opening both floors to the street, their attitude was one of respect for the building's large expanses of space, old stamped tin ceilings, and opportunities for daylight front, back, and through the roof. They even left exposed a concrete slab floor, which for some may be carrying respectfulness a little *too* far (although the floor does *look* handsome).

Another determinant was the designers' attitude toward display. Mauri's mandate was that the customers should be comfortable in the store and should be presented with merchandise in a plausible way. The museumlike settings appropriate for a closed showroom would have seemed unnaturally austere, it was thought, for a store wanting to welcome retail customers. What the designers devised, instead, is a series of freestanding display vignettes, each with a natural combination of

furniture and accessories, and each complete down to such details as groceries on the storage unit, a dressing gown on the bed, and half-empty wineglasses on the coffee table. However much such techniques may owe to "street theater" window displays or stage sets—an impression reinforced by the stands of undisguised theatrical lighting—they are refreshing newcomers to furniture stores. These vignettes need space around them, of course, to make them readable as isolated units. This means that only about half the items stocked by Abitare can be on the floor at one time. Displays are therefore constantly being changed, and Mauri considers this a virtue. "We want people to know," he says, "that when they come back next week, they'll see something else."

Abitare, in almost every respect, has gone its own spirited way. Mauri is looking at new sites in Washington, D.C., and Houston; within three years, he thinks, there will be at least six Abitare stores in the United States. If the others are as visually striking as the first, taking as many chances and succeeding as often, they will be very welcome.

(Above) One of the 10-ft (3-m) high lighting masts. View of open stair (above left) through "pinstripe" wire glass of conference room.

Under a row of skylights, a view towards the exposed steel truss at the second floor window.

CONRAN'S, NEW YORK

Shoppers can spot Conran's the proverbial mile away. Merchandise rises to mountainous heights from spacious selling floors in attractive displays that invite close physical examination. Prices are moderate. Yet the general level of product design is surprisingly high. As for the interior design: it is the merchandise itself, with only plain tiled floors, white walls, discreet signage, and track lighting for its stage setting.

All this represents the thinking of Terence Conran, the forty-seven-year old chairman and major shareholder of the Habitat Group based in Wallingford, United Kingdom, and his colleagues. Trained and experienced as an industrial designer of far-ranging interests, Conran conceived the idea of a chain of stores retailing well-designed contemporary home furnishings that represent good value for the money. The first of Europe's Habitats opened in London in 1964.

The first Conran's, as the North American operation of Habitat is known, is a 40,000-sq-ft (3,717½-m²) store in New York's Citicorp Center (see pages 134–137), designed by Conran Associates Ltd., architects, and Andrew Blackman, associate architect, which opened early in 1978. Like its European counterparts, Conran's is a celebration of unfettered Miesian space. "Customers need room to move around," says Michael Tyson, president of Conran's. "To us, they're as important as the merchandise." So space stretches everywhere, free of ceiling and floor-level changes or partitions. A perusal of Conran's two floors—a rectangular space at street level which carries the main furntiure department on one-third of the store's total floor area, and a roughly U-shaped second floor, with KD furniture, window, wall, and flooring departments, kitchenwares, bed and bath accessories, china, glass, toys, and lighting, wrapped around the huge skylit atrium of Citicorp's three-story Market—reveals them to be as intensely cultivated as rice paddies.

Customers are pulled in from street-level entrances on the sidewalk and within the Market through the furniture floor and upstairs on a closed-loop path designed for maximum exposure and minimum security risk. Checkout counters and shopping carts lend a calculated air of supermarket merchandising

The interior design at Conran's, the complete home furnishing store at New York's Citicorp Center, consists of merchandise in mountainous peaks, soldiered rows, and casual vignettes. Views here show the toy department (opposite page). Mssrs. Tyson and Conran (top), and various other departments in the 40,000-sq-ft (3,717½-m²) store.

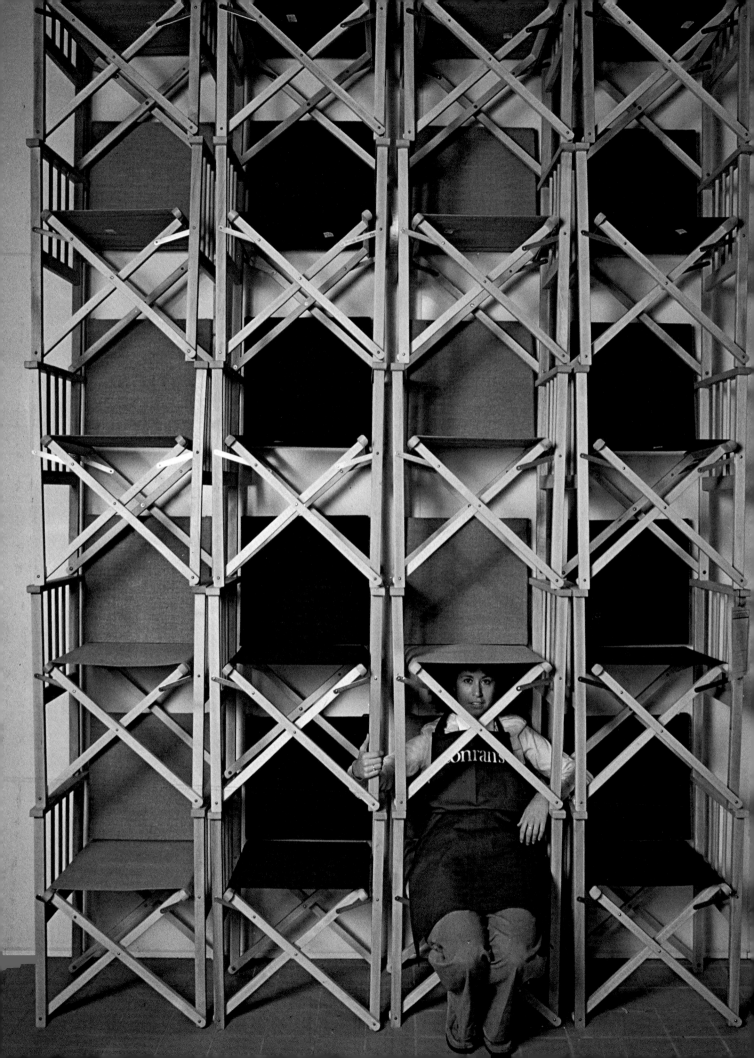

to the store. Floor plans and space allocations are studied and shifted with the seasons. Changing the displays refreshes customer interest—and display is the genius of Conran's interiors. Since the product range is relatively small (some 4,500 lines) and stable (some items have been carried since 1964), Conran's manipulates the elements of its interior design to emphasize product availability (stock is actually "warehoused" on the selling floor), low cost with quality (great quantities seen in dramatic lighting), and accessibility (customers may handle merchandise).

Tungsten spot lighting, costly but warm in color, set against a neutral ceiling of white enameled metal channels and tile flooring, draws attention to islands of merchandise whose dimensions violate the traditional "eye-level" visual zone of retailing. Rather than concentrate the customer's focal plane, Conran's diffuses it. Up, down, everywhere is merchandise. Though the overall impression is still of precise order, the customers cannot possibly see and understand the full product range at a glance, or even after a few visits. This is exactly what Conran's wants. As Tyson points out, "Our average customer returns once every three weeks to spend three-fourths of an hour, a high amount of time devoted to a store. Since only 50 percent of the customers actually buy, it is wise to leave them with the feeling that new items are waiting to be discovered. You didn't see it all? Come again!"

Display is high art at Conran's. Note wide range of merchandise for home use, pick-up baskets, and clerk's apron (coordinated with shopping carts not shown), which reinforce supermarket image, and use of form and color to create interest in the neutral interior.

CONRAN'S, NEW ROCHELLE, NEW YORK

The "supermarket" concept of letting goods speak for themselves is the secret of Conran's design and merchandising formula and a vital part of a seventeen-year-old success story, another chapter of which opened in 1979 in New Rochelle, New York. The 20,000-sq-ft (1, 859-m²) home furnishings store is the second to be opened in the United States by Conran's. The interior design, a product of Conran Associates, differs little from that of Conran's first American store, in Manhattan's Citicorp Center (see pages 22–25). The tile floors, white walls, and track lighting are much the same—that is, they create a neutral background for the display of merchandise. Design is not allowed to detract from the inherent appeal of the goods themselves.

The current vogue for incorporating food into retail design is reflected in the addition of a coffee bar that is tucked away in a corner of the store; according to American president Michael Tyson, it is doing a land-office business.

Conran's supermarket concept of merchandising, combining a small product range with availability—both of which serve to keep prices down—has also been brilliantly translated into a $2, 112-page color catalog. Requests for it are coming in at the rate of 1,000 per day. That the catalog provides an aesthetic experience much like that of walking through the store speaks highly of Conran's design team, which is able to apply the "Conran formula" to the printed page and the interior space with equal success. At the bottom of it all, however, is the philosophy expressed so well by Tyson: "We don't want people to see a beautiful store; we do want them to see beautiful merchandise." The firm plans to open another twenty stores on the East Coast in the next five years, proving that the no-frills approach has a secure spot in the marketplace.

CHARRETTE

The Charrette architectural supply store on East 54th Street in New York City is an attractive alteration of a boring, standard commercial space. Produced on a rather tight budget by architect Max Bier of Bier, Baxt and Hirsch, the store functions as a horizontal arrangement in a building that is basically a deep box.

The exposed ceiling, visible verification of an elderly proverb lauding necessity as the mother of invention, is the positive offspring of the shoestring budget. For the ceiling itself, with its pipes and enormous ducts, has become a major architectural element. The largest duct, used for air conditioning, accents the space, lending visual interest in its "round-versus-square" attitude. The shifted-axis plan also helps to offset the strong horizontal pull.

There is an interesting transition between the ceiling and the other major element of interest, the curved wall, in that a pipe is bent to follow the configuration of the wall. Track lighting is then attached to the straighter portions of the pipe, killing two turkeys with one well-aimed stone. The wall performs the added function of providing necessary screening for the office space. Bunkerlike slots enable employees to observe shoppers'

needs and movements.

Essentially a hardware store of graphic arts, with accents of polished design, Charrette comes off as a highly successful combination of diamonds and blue jeans. Of more importance, it works. A long wall of standard industrial shelving faces the front counter, which operates in a dual capacity. It serves as an attractive, bar-height display counter in front; behind, it houses hundreds of drawers for the storage of small items. The front of the store is designed and stocked for quicker sales; in the rear, in areas that are apt to be congested because of the nature of the items on display, there is extra space for milling about. An important consideration of the store is that all items, large and small, always be visible.

The rear of the store, given over to larger items such as drafting tables, has an existing skylight, which allows for natural light, and a dropped ceiling, which adds intimacy to the space and houses the air-conditioning system. From this room a staircase leads to a small, vaultlike conference room with a serving pantry, a space useful as a lunchroom and for product or design seminars. An adjacent building, also part of the store, is used for bulk storage and as a shipping area.

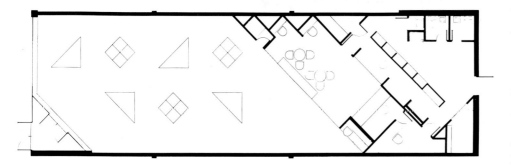

Floor Plan 2800 sq.ft.

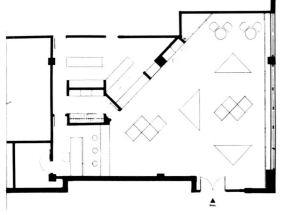

Floor Plan 1700 sq.ft.

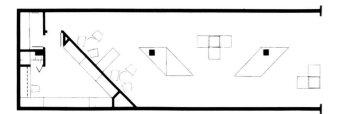

Floor Plan 1320 sq.ft.

Plans for retail outlets of three different sizes and shapes illustrate how the basic vocabulary of display elements can be adapted to a variety of conditions.

AT&T

A century-old monopoly has ended. Until recently, those of us who used the vast telephone network of the American Telephone & Telegraph Company also, as a matter of course, rented our telephones from AT&T. For about a decade, however, it has been possible to buy, rather than lease, telephones, provided that the purchaser pay AT&T for a "protective device" with which to attach the instrument. Now, because of an order of the Federal Communications Commission, we are free to buy and install any phone we choose.

This developing liberalization of the telephone market has, naturally, brought corresponding developments in sales techniques. Independent telephone manufacturers are delighted about their future possibilities, but AT&T is by no means pessimistic: Charles L. Brown, AT&T's president, has announced his intention to be highly competitive.

One manifestation of this new competitiveness has been the unveiling, by AT&T and others, of new telephone designs. For the most part, except for those who may lose their hearts to a Mickey Mouse model, these elaborate concoctions exemplify industrial design at its overwrought worst.

Very different and very much more encouraging are the prototype retail store designs commissioned by AT&T from the firm of Robert P. Gersin Associates. Two of the stores are planned or already in operation in Florida, two in upstate New York, three in New Jersey, and four in Ohio. Some of these are renovations of existing spaces; some are new. All are in locations, such as shopping centers, that have strong neighborhood ties.

In these stores, potential customers can see various telephone styles and colors, learn how different telephones and accessories operate (by means of tape recordings, the telephones actually talk to those who pick them up), learn what services and rates are available, and—perhaps most radical of all—make their selections on the spot and take their telephones home to plug in for immediate use.

The flexible design elements are planned to encourage independent customer "browsing" without constant attendance; the time that service representatives must spend with customers is therefore minimized. Triangular display units are adaptable to any suitably sized space—from 1,500 to 3,000 sq ft (139½ to 279 m²)—and display panels can easily be added or eliminated.

There are provisions as well for paying telephone bills and requesting repairs to existing telephone services. In short, these facilities will make AT&T a directly accessible neighborhood presence. Illustrations here are of the earliest prototype outlets, but such stores will eventually be built all across the country. As far as the Gersin design is concerned, however, success is already apparent.

Store facades and graphic design, as well as interior arrangements, were important parts of the Gersin design. A giant "hello" silk-screened just inside one store's entrance is both welcoming and suggestive of phone use.

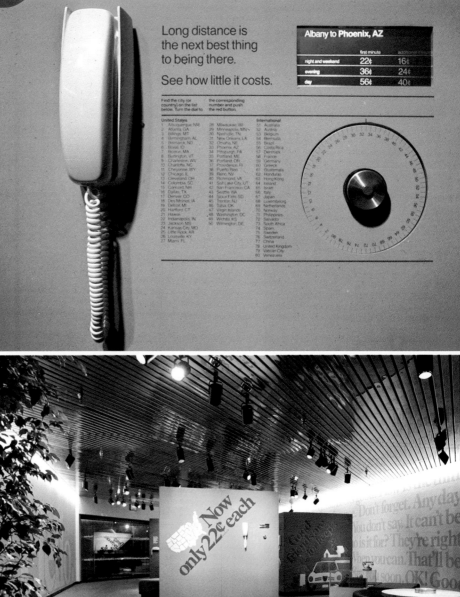

Public areas of the retail outlets seen in six views here provide displays and explanations of equipment types, panels for actual demonstrations (phones are wired to tape recorders in the rear of the stores), and counters for business transactions. Ceilings throughout are of reflective aluminum strips, establishing a diagonal grid for the displays below.

33

80 WEST 40TH STREET, NEW YORK

Give New York realtors their way, and "McKim, Mead & White Slept Here" would be chiseled on every prewar building facade—though it really doesn't matter for buildings like 80 West 40th Street. The occupants of this Beaux Arts structure on the periphery of Bryant Park and the city's famous Garment District have taken up the cause of its delightfully idiosyncratic interiors, transforming many into unique contemporary designs that deftly incorporate the building's venerable old forms. Interior designs by Alice Blaine, Martin Green, Bill Polito, and Carmelo Pomodoro are featured here.

Since opening its doors as the Beaux Arts Apartments in 1876, 80 West 40th Street has enjoyed a busy if checkered career. Gracious duplex and triplex apartments, a business address for ladies of easy virtue, photographers' studios, sound-recording labs—

they have all passed through at some time. It is the designers of apparel and fabric who have elevated the building to its resplendent new state.

In 1973 the fashion house of Jonathan Logan was persuaded to move in and ultimately possess three floors. These interiors were occupied in a strictly utilitarian spirit by the firm's designers. Then came a crop of "hot" young designers like Alice Blaine, whose bold interior design for her penthouse showroom-workroom-office set a fast, stylish pace. Says David Wilshin, secretary-treasurer of Sutton & Towne, realtors, and manager of 80 West 40th Street, "The building has been radically transformed. Those designers invest in their interior designs, and we support them with new elevators, sprinklers, code compliance, and renovation." He is obviously proud of the building.

Alice Blaine studio (pictured here) places simple furnishings in airy space.

Alice Blaine: Alice Blaine. Visitors to the "Greenhouse" on the top floor find themselves in an aviary designed by Alice Blaine to accommodate her growing fashion business. This tour de force makes brilliant use of natural light, two-story elevations, indoor plants, and extremely simple furnishings to produce an interior that manages to be spacious and intimate at the same time—and a far cry from what a sound-recording lab left behind.

"Most designers work in rat holes," Blaine says. "There was nothing here when I arrived. No floor, no windows, no ceiling at all.

Every surface was painted black. It was pretty raw."

After demolition, Blaine opened the space with a skylight in the mansard roof, windows along the wall facing Bryant Park, a large mirror screen in the bay facing the windows, and white paint everywhere. A loft to one end of the space was converted from a control room to a workroom. Plaster Grecian orders (including fluted piers with capitals and entablatures, moldings, and a frieze reproduced from the Parthenon) were lovingly restored. Plants were carefully chosen for appearance (as room dividers) and for their ability to sur-

vive. Outdoor furniture (to seat buyers in four selling areas), slab-sided desks with Kevi desk chairs (for administrative work), industrial lockers (to hold clothing for presentation), industrial lighting (to give general illumination and lower the ceiling to a more human scale), and a custom mezzanine platform constructed from stock metal parts by many manufacturers (upon which sits Blaine's own office, below which are racks of clothes) complete the design.

"It's really a landscape," Blaine says. "Everything is kept mobile"—a sensible idea for a company on the move.

Martin Greene: Imprints. A magnificent Gothic-style fireplace is the focal point of the interior design by Martin Greene for Imprints, his fabric house. Strong contrast is provided by downlighting cylinders in the exposed-beam ceiling, parquet flooring, and nearly self-effacing tables and chairs. Fabric in baskets, fabric in bolts against the walls, and fabric in rolls in a colorful fabric storage wall dominate this subdued arrangement, as they should.

Carmelo Pomodoro: Stan Herman Studio. Under the aegis of a Gothic-style pendant vaulted ceiling and a balcony with friezes in the style of Luca della Robbia, Carmelo Pomodoro was quite content to clean and restore original plaster details, and then to create an interior of simple white furniture, Breuer Cesca chairs, industrial lights, and an antique armoire for his employer, the fashion studio of Stan Herman. Although the space is relatively small, the floor plan seems more generous than it really is because of a 45° grid. Wood floors and bright red upholstery warm austere white surfaces.

Imprints (above) uses fabric to impart color and texture to rooms. Stan Herman Studio (above left) contrasts rich bas-relief with elemental furniture forms and splashes of bright red upholstery. Liz Claiborne (opposite page) revolves about pyramid for clothing displays.

Bill Polito: Liz Claiborne. Hovering over the center of the showroom floor at the showroom-workroom-office of Liz Claiborne by interior designer Bill Polito is (you guessed it) a pyramid. Polito knows what he's doing; having worked with clothing designer Liz Claiborne and her husband and business partner, Art Ortenberg, on previous occasions, Polito was well qualified to create a new, larger facility in the same building housing his earlier design for them. The result is an interior of charm, simplicity, and utility carried out to the smallest details.

"They made my work a pleasure," says Polito of his clients. "They had a good sense of how all their activities related that enabled us to work together efficiently. And Liz, being the great designer and colorist she is, recognized what she wanted at once."

Polito divided the space into showroom, reception area, office and conference room, workroom, and rest rooms, with the existing balcony level providing a natural separation of activities. Each space has its own individual characteristics of size, form, color, and texture. The showroom relaxes with three casual seating groups for buyers and a sweater bin flanking the pyramid in the center of a hardwood floor. A heavy-duty Pirelli rubber tile floor and clean-cut casework set off an existing staircase in the concise reception area. Office and conference room are appropriately carpeted and furnished with storage, work surfaces, and a fabric-covered wall for tacking (the firm is fond of graphs).

About that pyramid. "It came early in the project," says Polito. "Liz wanted many activities in the center of the showroom, and the means for modeling, displaying, and storing clothing for three simultaneous presentations." The KD structure comes equipped with doors, hanging rods, mirrors, and casters. Besides roaming about the floor (or folding up for full showings to a packed house), allowing staff to pop in and out for quick changes and additional merchandise, and providing a neutral backdrop for presentations, the pyramid imparts an air of drama and monumentality to the room. Polito's pyramid is a living one.

A cut of another cloth. Four talented designers could be expected to produce four distinctive interior designs, and such is the case at 80 West 40th Street. What similarities there are evolved independently from basic needs of the fashion industry, that is, efficient use of expensive floor space, simple furnishings that stress comfort and utility, workrooms apart from (but convenient to) showrooms, and lighting and color schemes that enhance fabric and clothing but do not overwhelm them. For all their intrinsic interest, the four interiors are subordinate to this end. "Obviously," says Alice Blaine, "I want to sell clothes here."

An innocent-looking "puddle of a creek" that courses almost unnoticed through Cross Country Plaza, Kansas City, Missouri, became a raging flood on the night of September 12, 1977, devastating the fashionable Moorish-style shopping center. One of the most distinguished victims was Hall's Plaza, whose management vowed to reopen in time for its sixty-third consecutive Christmas season. Thanks to the company's determination, the services of Harper & George, architectural and industrial designers (see their World Trade Center restaurants, pages 138–143), and the cooperation of Hall's many suppliers, the "miracle" came true.

Hall's, a wholly owned subsidiary of the Hallmark organization, has been known to Kansas City since 1914 as a purveyor of the finest-quality traditional lines of porcelain, crystal, silverware, jewelry, stationery, and other gifts and decorative accessories. Natu-

rally, its interior design has always upheld this image. Shoppers who visited it just prior to the flood saw a contemporary setting graced with classic references and rich appointments in onyx, hardwoods, and other costly materials.

The flood obliterated this interior and all Hall's stock as well, giving Harper & George a *tabula rasa* to redesign, fabricate, and install in six breathless weeks. The firm's solution: a space-frame and storage system, constructed offsite in readily available material, capable of change and variation, and easily assembled—in effect, an interior design nearly independent of the building shell.

Management initially questioned the "systems" approach as being overly utilitarian for the ambience needed to sell its merchandise. As it turned out, Harper & George's interpretation of the systems concept for Hall's was both ingeniously pragmatic and reas-

suringly handsome. Construction had to be specified for fast processing, so the designer called for individual display pavilions comprising wood studs with 3-by-3-in. (7½-by-7½-cm) and 2-by-4-in. (5-by-10-cm) sections, and birch plywood baffles, gusseting, and shelving finished with light sanding and flame-resistant spray, industrial pendant lighting, and colorful fabric panels and banners for space definition and signage.

Erection was so fast—two weeks—that Hall's reopened three days ahead of schedule. Each pavilion arrived with its own jigs and patterns to be bolted together in Erector Set fashion. The long power cords of the lighting pendants were connected into existing high-hat outlets using adapters, effectively lowering the visual plane from 13½ ft (4 m) to the new, smaller scale of the wood system. (Accent lighting is standard photographic clip-on fixtures attached to the shelving.) A soft,

Temporary wood structural system by Harper & George for Hall's Plaza is put through its paces in these views. (Opposite page) System combined with graphic banners and industrial pendant lighting fixtures creates miniature pavilions for china, flatware, table serving pieces, and bath linen. Stretched fabric forms tents over clothing racks (left). (Above) Arcade of banners announces various departments.

unobtrusive color scheme was established by color-coding departments to the pastel banners that identify them; the banners, suspended over the central circulation corridor formed by a freestanding "trellis" of wood struts, provide a colorful invitation to walk through the entire store. The ceiling was painted black, but otherwise left much as it once was.

On opening day, Hall's staff promptly observed that the store had never looked so spacious before. Curiously enough, this phenomenon coincided with a net *reduction* in selling-floor area. An interior design of space frames rather than walls and a lighting design that focuses on products rather than architecture obscures the physical boundaries once defined by partitions, making store fixtures and products float like stars of a summer nighttime sky. The effect politely conceals the fact that stock once stored in the basement is now kept on the periphery of the main floor. Studs 2 ft (½ m) on center carry baffles and adjustable shelving for storage and display.

Of course, the most conspicuous change in Hall's is its new spirit. Bold banners, natural wood, and modern fixtures with an architectural character have introduced the store and its quality consumer lines to a younger, more style-conscious segment of the consumer market without alienating Hall's traditional customers. No one could regard the flood as beneficent—but Hall's has survived the sea change, and the brave new world before it looks very inviting.

These perspectives illustrate why the interior looks larger despite net reduction in selling floor space. Structural system, directed lighting plots, darkened ceiling, and strategically placed banners tend to soften actual boundary edges of building shell. Note such devices as banners in clothing department (right), which conceal fascia and soffit where ceiling height drops; lack of strong building forms to compete with presentation of merchandise; use of lighting pendants to establish lower visual plane than existing ceiling to concentrate customers' attention.

BULLOCK'S, SAN JOSE, CALIFORNIA

When Bullock's of Northern California decided to build a new store in San Jose's Oakridge Mall, board chairman Paul Heidrick cited three priorities: energy savings, innovative design, and new merchandising techniques. The key to all three problems was found in the use of a Teflon-coated Fiberglas fabric roof, believed to be the first one used in a department store. The architect, Environmental Planning & Research, Inc. (EPR), of San Francisco, covered the center third of the store's upper level, about 16,000 sq ft (1,487 m²), with a double layer of the fabric, which is supported by four laminated wood arches.

To date, the energy savings have been impressive. Since the store's opening in the fall of 1978, electrical consumption has registered as little as 150,900 kilowatt-hours per month, and Bullock's foresees a yearly energy savings of approximately $18,000. The translucent fabric roof reduces the need for daytime artificial illumination and the resulting need of air conditioning to combat the heat generated by those lights. The two layers of fabric reduce heat transfer, and the inner layer absorbs noise. The fabric is resistant to fire, moisture, ultraviolet light degradation, and thermal expansion. The Teflon coating makes it virtually self-cleaning.

The roof has created new design and merchandising possibilities as well. The area under it is column-free, allowing for greater design flexibility. The lighting, suspended from a yellow space frame, can be arranged to focus on display areas at night, while circulation and nonselling areas can be left more dimly lit. This location was chosen for the housewares and gifts section, as this merchandise is best displayed under natural light. With generous use of plantings, the designers have created a solariumlike atmosphere. On the strength of this store's success, Bullock's is examining the possibility of an entirely fabric-covered store.

43

What occupies four lively and colorful floors, is the talk of Philadelphia, cost just $10 per square foot, and was planned, designed and constructed in six fast and furious months? Ask Edward Secon, designer of 1610 Chestnut Street in Philadelphia, the new retail store combining the Workbench, the Pottery Barn, Fabrications, Rittenhouse Carpet, and It's a Small World under the roof of a former men's clothier. "Contemplation is a luxury you can seldom afford in store design," says Secon. "When other designers are refining renderings, models, and presentations, you're completing the job. It takes just as much skill—but you've got to show it fast."

The clients at 1610 Chestnut Street left him little time to spare. Warren Rubin, president of the Workbench chain of contemporary furniture stores, wanted the four-story 1927 Art Deco building being vacated by Jackson & Moyer, a prestigious men's clothier, to house his expanding Philadelphia operation. Its 34,000 sq ft (3,160 m²) exceeded his needs, however. But if other tenants retailing compatible merchandise could be persuaded to share the space. . . .

R. Hoyt Chapin and Walton Brush, co-owners of the Pottery Barn chain of household specialty stores, and Peter-Ayres Tarantino, manager and president of the venture capital group sponsoring the Philadelphia Pottery Barn and Fabrications, expressed strong interest. In a matter of months, the concept of a retail store offering comprehensive and cohesive lines of household furnishings and accessories evolved, whereby all five retail activities would share the same space, each prorated for a given floor area.

So the race to occupancy was on. "Considering that some clients ask me for a complete store from scratch in four weeks' time, I wasn't surprised by this project," Secon comments. Beyond the need to rebuild completely the not-too-solid wood plank floors, install an additional elevator, and preserve and restore the original Art Deco facade, he made quick work of the existing structure.

Charming though the exterior was, the interior of Jackson & Moyer was not particularly remarkable. Light fixtures and classic columns at street level were retained and played against the austere, almost Shakerlike simplicity Secon has given other Pottery Barns as their standard: that is, white walls; naturally finished wood floors, shelving, and display fixtures; isolated light plots in a field of lowered general light distribution; and controlled passages of raw open space for such vignettes as table settings, lounge seating groups, and special displays. Pottery Barn merchandise dominates one side of the floor, shown to advantage with Workbench furniture, table dressage by Fabrications, and rugs and wall hangings by Rittenhouse Carpet.

A high ceiling at street level suggested a mezzanine above, so Secon framed an H-shaped plane into the existing structural system that visitors enter by stairs at the far end of the store. To protect the integrity of the facade, the mezzanine soffit is stepped back to reveal its independence. It forms a shaded, intimate space that proved to be a most appro-

Project renovation is politely concealed outside, strongly stated inside. Facade (below) is original, with display enclosures removed to reveal store interior. Entrance (below right) is two-story space framed by mezzanine. Note 1610 Chestnut St. graphics on directory. Floor displays and merchandise fixtures (opposite page) freely intermingle on main floor.

Upper levels of store continue loose flowing spaces (opposite page, below). Second level (above and opposite page, above) has simple casework to form rectilinear solids and lighting troughs. Third level (right and opposite page, below) adapts existing forms with paint and lighting to dramatize toys and furnishings.

Store's special charm is merchandise it-self—on display racks, arranged in vi-gnettes, casually stacked and scattered like a country store. Stairway (below) leads to mezzanine space for Fabrications (opposite page, below right). Dining setting awaits customers (opposite page, above right).

priate setting for the Fabrications collections of imported and domestic fabrics.

Secon's solution for the second level is rather ingenious. Given an existing fluorescent lighting system and an anonymous warehouse of a space, he created channeled luminaires, painted yellow inside, that frame the lamps into the structural columns to impart a warm glow to the room. A large cube at the base of each column provides display space above and storage space inside for the KD furniture of Workbench. A wall of industrial windows facing Chestnut Street is left exposed to bring natural light inside, as are the street-level windows with their display enclosures removed to attract passersby. Simple wood and glass shelving with integral downlighting completes the space with its rough-hewn yet unexpectedly delicate texture.

The most ambitious design solutions of the Jackson & Moyer store are found on the third level, whose curving walls and undulating ceilings intrigued Secon by their potential for reuse. "It would have been cheaper to tear the whole thing down," he says. "But I couldn't resist experimenting. I selectively retained parts of the 1950s design to see what might result." He thus produced the unique selling floor for It's a Small World, the well-known Philadelphia retailer of contemporary imported and domestic toys, games, clothing, and accessories for children, shown with settings of children's furniture by Workbench. This is an appropriately capricious design, in which bright monochromatic colors articulate the surviving Mannerist shapes of the former interior. Although he enclosed the center to create a small, three-sided rectangular space for It's a Small World, Secon repeated the light and airy theme of the previous levels with large open spaces on the periphery of this room within a room, complemented by another wall of industrial windows.

Traffic has been so good since opening day that the store is considering the addition of a public staircase. Having designed everything down to the striking logo for the address that each retailer adapts to his own advertising, Secon is pleased but not very surprised. "This is the kind of store for people like me and my friends," he observes. "We're well educated, well traveled, and we like the look of Mies chairs—but can't always pay for the authentic details. This store affirms that we can have access to good design at reasonable prices. It's a celebration of mass production at its best."

Secon, a designer who creates furniture, lamps, and accessories as well as interiors, and Ben Lloyd, designer of the store's displays, can take a bow themselves, for 1610 Chestnut Street is a celebration of interior design that is graceful, concise, and eminently usable—at a price almost everyone can afford.

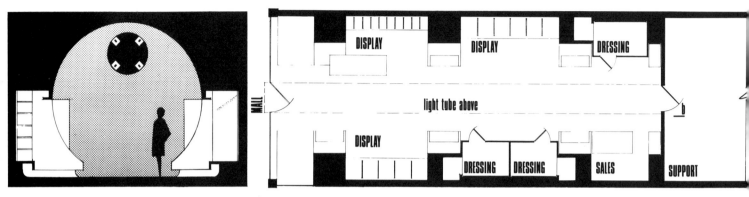

COURREGES BOUTIQUE

Courrèges was the first couturier to send his models onto the runway swinging tennis rackets instead of sauntering sedately. His crisp clothes epitomize the revolution in lifestyles that in the late sixties relegated *haute couture* to a backstage position in the fashion industry while propelling a new generation of Paris designers into ready-to-wear. It is no surprise that Courrèges's boutiques are among the most refreshingly designed shops selling French-made clothes to the American woman.

The Courrèges boutique in the magnificent Chestnut Hill Mall outside Boston is an apt translation of the Courrèges style into the vocabulary of interior design by Stull Associates, Inc., architects, and interior designer Jean Bottineau. The clean-cut geometric construction of Courrèges's clothes is echoed by the witty visual pun of using his initial C as the outline for a concentric hollow sculpture that encompasses the storefront, the main sign, the window and interior displays, the shelving for stock, the lighting, the air-conditioning ducts, and much of the seating in two structural elements. The first is the circular suspended tube—containing all the lighting fixtures and air-conditioning ducts, and faced with Courrèges's backlit, silhouetted AC logotype—which protrudes a few inches beyond the storefront. Among the advantages of this device is the fact that it permits visual and psychological perception of the full height of the space, unlike a height-eating dropped ceiling. The second is the C-contour outline of the interior space itself—a long tube. The surface of this tube extends at the front of the shop into winglike suspended tables actually fixed in position (the carpet rides up a few inches under them) but visually "floated" by base lighting. The built-in seating also flows from it, and the doors to the dressing rooms, office, and support room at the rear (where the seamstresses and fitters work) do not destroy the effect that it is a coherent, continuous structure.

White is Courrèges's favorite color; when correctly lighted, it makes a refreshing display background for the vivid hues and pure tints that Courrèges uses in his clothes. Every surface in the boutique that is not mirrored or made of stainless steel is white—painted plaster and wood, leather upholstery, and wool carpeting. Dexterous lighting makes the mirror-expanded space—actually only 1,500 sq ft (139½ m²)—glorious, not blinding. The white carpet, incidentally, is top quality in order to stand up to the required cleaning schedule (every other month).

Narcissism. Looking good is as important as feeling good these days, and the increasing sophistication of the salon client is reflected in design. No more pink plastic and French-poodle-patterned wallpaper. High design is the name of the game. But the ulterior motive remains the same: to make the customer feel pampered and special. In The Arrangement, a beauty salon in Palatine, Illinois, Chicago

architect Stanley Tigerman was faced with the challenge of creating a unique design in a narrow 80-by-20-ft (24-by-6-m) space, with an even narrower budget.

Tigerman used the space to the greatest possible advantage by creating facing double rows of styling booths, a design based on the concept of "stacking up" clients, as in a parking garage—shades of the assembly line, but

that is where the design aspect comes in. The materials used are simple—lots of plastic laminates and mirrors (the budget precluded anything more lavish)—but they are used with a free hand and a keen wit; the space is made special by the design forms. Sensuous, curving shapes greet the eye at every turn: in the partitions between booths, in the walls, and especially in the mirrors that line both walls.

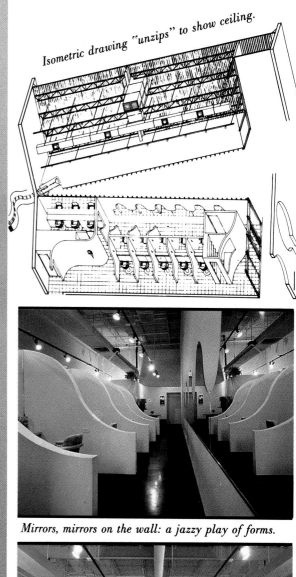

Isometric drawing "unzips" to show ceiling.

Mirrors, mirrors on the wall: a jazzy play of forms.

The mirrors' bell shape echoes the shape of the human head and shoulders. There are also mirrors over the styling counters, and these, in combination with the curved wall mirrors, create infinity readings, multiple views, and the opportunity for what architect Tigerman calls "lateral snooping"—a crucial part of the see-and-be-seen ambience of any salon.

Tigerman, a member of the "Chicago Eight" group of architects, is known for his sense of humor and sardonically witty designs, such as his project for the Federal Design Assembly in which government offices were given partitions made of stacks of regulation paper bound together with red tape. Here, Tigerman's lavish use of mirrors makes an ironic comment on the state of self-indulgence in the Me Generation.

On the practical side, the entire cost of the project, including fixtures and equipment, weighed in at a tiny $25,000. The clients, Barbara Walker and Linda Burdeen, obtained space in the Prairie Brook Commercial Building, also a Tigerman product, but their funds were limited. Rather than regarding this as a handicap, Tigerman saw it as a stimulus to greater resourcefulness and creativity.

JANICE JULIAN

Being nimble in what may be very tight spaces has been a special resource of Israeli-born architect Ari Bahat. When he came to the United States in the late 1960s as a member of an Israeli dance group, Bahat liked the audience enough to stay. The architecture he found here was often pared to the essentials, leaving him a palette of commonplace materials to exploit in limited spaces as best he could. His design for Janice Julian, a New York hair salon, is a superb example of what a lean budget and strong creativity can accomplish.

"I started the design process with a program," says Bahat, "although many owners want to begin with a design. Then came the plan." It would be difficult to imagine his handling Janice Julian any other way. The existing space needed a decisive plan: the room was long and narrow with a bulge at one end; an unwanted two-story ceiling was only partially covered by a balcony over the "bulge"; the floor sloped; there were two entrances to control, from the street and from the building lobby; there was no air conditioning.

In this less than inviting shell Janice Julian wanted five work stations, three shampoo stations, a reception area, changing rooms, and storage. Though a first-time entrepreneur, Julian knew her business well. It would begin with a small staff serving business people in semiprivate settings with an atmosphere of understated modern elegance.

Bahat took advantage of the "bulge" by clustering the work stations in its center. He then surrounded them with the shampoo room, storage area, and changing rooms, defining everything in a series of 7-ft (2-m)-high partitions whose pivotal point is a reception area commanding visual control of both entrances. To dramatize the activities and tone down the building, he finished work stations and partitions in brushed aluminum laminate and set them against black enameled walls. He added further embellishment in the form of earthen floor tile, a reflective ceiling, plants, special lighting, and executive-style salon chairs in bright red upholstery.

Everything shows Bahat's close attention to function. The work station cluster is an imaginative use of cabinetry that encloses each customer with two projecting "fins" of its pinwheel configuration, bathes the space in soft, flattering light from overhead light boxes, and readily equips each stylist with the tools of the trade (enclosed cabinet, drying lamp, dryer and curler on retractable cords, telephone jack, and slots for bottles and other paraphernalia). The tile flooring is easy to clean. Because of the extensive use of built-in cabinetry, the salon always looks neat.

And customers like the space. Bahat's subdued color scheme of black and silver planes accented by green plants and red upholstery lends a surprisingly sophisticated air to such modest dimensions. This spirit should be sustained for a long time. Thanks to Bahat's bold design, there is still plenty of room for dancing—or, for that matter, three to four more work stations on the main floor, and services such as facial massage and manicure on the balcony.

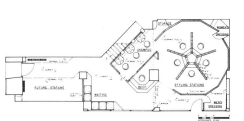

Views of Janice Julian revolve around the cluster of five work stations at the heart of the salon's operations (opposite page). Note spare use of color, offset by strong forms, reflective surfaces, subtle lighting, and bright red salon chairs. Entrance (top) and plan (left).

JULIO

People in hairdressing salons need a special atmosphere. They must be soothed and pampered, delighted and surprised by the surroundings. In the process of being groomed, you do not look your best; therefore, you need an environment that provides subtle enhancements. Lots of tricks are on hand to generate all those qualities in this salon, one of the shops within The Mayfair in the Grove shopping complex in Coconut Grove, Florida (see pages 130–133).

Dennis Abbé, who created the interior design, began his career as an illustrator and sees himself as an architectural artist. He believes in developing "meaning with fantasy." In this case, he wanted to emphasize the Florida location, so he devised a seascape theme. "Everybody knows Florida as a state for underwater adventures. This design calls up Captain Nemo *20,000 Leagues Under the Sea.*" The theme begins on the exterior of the salon, where black mosaic tiles form a glittering, shiny, serpentine shape below the shop windows. Each window, tilted on an angle, is etched with an Abbé design of aquatic

sirens and other sea creatures. Inside the shop, these windows become the hairdressing mirrors; all surfaces are tinted apricot to make the reflections more attractive and glowing. Underfoot, the floor is hand-painted with underwater motifs, the design transferred onto 2-by-4-ft (½-by-1-m) sections of vinyl and finished with two coats of industrial sealer. At other strategic points there are etched glass goldfish bowls, glass panels, and mirrors, all with marine connections, sparkling against dark vinyl walls. "Encrustaceans are everywhere," declares Abbé, whose description is as decorative as his design.

With silver-leaf paper overhead and wonderful peachy suede vinyl-upholstered curved banquettes, plus a flotilla of shiny black vinyl grooming chairs, the hairdressing salon is the nearest thing to an underwater grotto in dryland design terms. If it is theatrical, that is exactly the intention. Abbé says, "To me there is a textural rightness in this."

To Mr. and Mrs. Julio Marsell, the salon's Venezuelan owners, there is a rightness in terms of business. Theirs is a unisex operation, and the chairs are never empty. Both men and women are stimulated to return for elegant grooming over and over again.

SCHULLIN

Located in Vienna at *Graben 26*, the jewel shop Schullin by Hans Hollein adds a new luster to this elegant and historic shopping street. The shop's opening gesture is a brilliant, lightninglike cleft in the granite street wall which appears to strike the shimmering entrance door.

The fissure begins as a thin rivulet of brass, set shallowly in the highly polished granite surface of the upper facade. It widens imperceptibly as it falls, then breaks open, and appears to penetrate the solid granite, in cascading layers of overlapping metal (actually falsework over an existing cornice) for a depth of about 6 ft (2 m). As the penetration deepens, it narrows, and the metal lining darkens around a grouping of functional bright steel tubes (air conditioning) and lights; the overlapping layers also serve as louvers for fresh air intake. Subtly the penetration metamorphoses into a lovely door of exquisite workmanship (repeating in softened outline the form of the fissure) that beckons without revealing the inner chamber.

The interior of the 7-by-20-ft (2-by-6-m) shop, hardly as large as a stateroom, is fitted simply and luxuriously. Colors are dark and surfaces soft and inviting. As Hollein remarks, "Both in visual and in haptical sensations, there is a connection of the room with the product." The only jewellike surface, however, is the highly polished granite side wall. The "lost" space within it is used for discreet illuminated cases where jewels are highly visible but perfectly secure.

The ceiling height is used to every advantage to enlarge the room. The space narrows as it rises, in a geometric repetition of the outline of the fissure, which also serves to conceal ductwork. Two small, finely detailed counters, as well as the inner surface of the door, are paneled in leather and bound with brass. The furniture is cherry wood and brown plastic. Floor, walls, and ceiling planes, in contrast to the hardness of the granite, are all soft, brown, velourlike surfaces.

At the back of the shop is a minuscule office, concealed by a velvet curtain. Overhead at the ceiling apex a twin row of light globes in long steel sockets (rendered fourfold by reflection in the granite) slips through the looking glass—and continues to infinity.

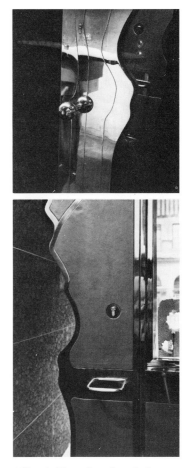

(Above) Two details of the entrance door: a spherical knob on the brass exterior face and a horizontal pull on the brass-and-velour interior.

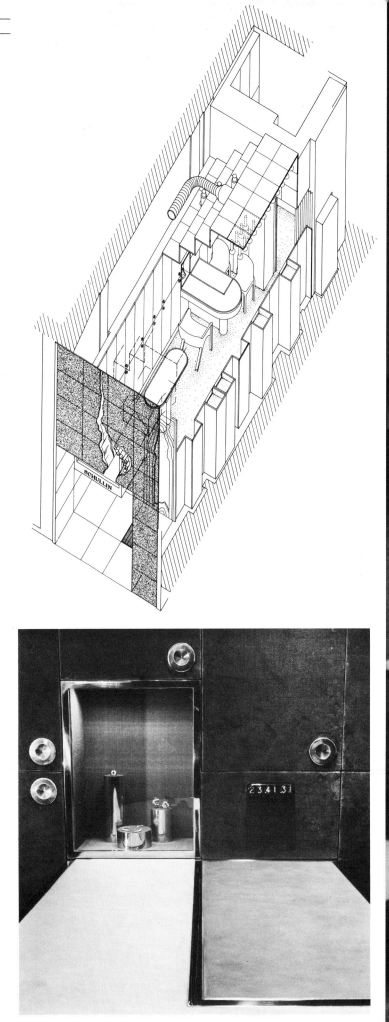

(Opposite page, below) A leather counter top, edged with brass, aligns with a small display case set into the velour-paneled storage wall. (Left) Looking toward the entrance from the rear of the shop; ceiling lights are reflected in the polished granite wall.

61

BULGARI JEWELLERS DANAOS LTD.

In 1971 the Bulgari brothers, Nicola, Paolo, and Gianni, decided to tuck the New York branch of their elegant and prestigious jewelry business into a quiet corner of the Hotel Pierre on Fifth Avenue. This boutique approach was so successful that in 1975 additional space was contracted for, including adjoining areas in the Getty Building on Madison Avenue. The design by Piero Sartogo, of Sartogo Architects and Associates of Rome, is understated, yet projects an atmosphere of uniqueness and elegance that complements the gems and the very special clientele attracted by them.

The entrance to the shop at the northeast corner of the hotel is at once severe and compelling. Clear glass, mirror, brass, and chrome are combined to create an inviting foyer that teases your interest even when you realize that you may not enter until a guard releases the handsome gate of basket-woven brass and chrome.

Mirror continues to play a large part in the design of the interior spaces. The baseboard and picture molding areas are both of mirror, the latter providing the major lighting as it is punctuated by custom-cut-crystal rods that carry light from thirty parr bulbs concealed behind them. This strip of mirror and lighted crystal also houses the many hidden TV cameras. Corners of the display rooms are mirrored on one side from ceiling to floor, encompassing recessed and lighted display cases or doors to the next area.

As though floating, the walls, framed by mirrors, are of special interest. They gleam on their own with a high-gloss clear finish over ¼-in. (6¼-mm) blocks of curly maple that have been bleached with acid three or four times and then laminated in a herringbone pattern to panels of plywood. The subdued color is complemented by the wall-to-wall carpet of the same hue, and the glossy finish again recalls the elegance of the chrome and brass entrance.

No particular period of design is prominent. The display desks and tables are antique writing tables and custom showcases with the herringbone treatment on the aprons and carpeted pedestals, all designed with special input from Gianni Bulgari. The chairs, designed by Ward Bennett, are customized in a soft raspberry-red aniline finish. The table lamps, specially designed by Mario Miqueli, provide both fluorescent and incandescent lighting from beneath traditional silk shades.

The muted colors and elegant textures in this handsome shop make you feel very much at home, or at least as though you would be if you could afford the merchandise.

Featured in the mirrored corners of each room are displays like this one (above). A contemporary display table (top), with carpeted base and herringbone case top, is equally at home in the sales areas. Mirrors everywhere (left) reflect the quiet opulence and expand the spaces which are all without benefit of daylight.

RESTAURANTS

Dining out today can be a very confusing experience, from the standpoint of design. Restaurants have long been an arena for design experimentation and innovation, but the variations are more numerous now than ever before. This is in no small part a result of the modern view of restaurants as marketable commodities, like clothing and furniture. The atmosphere is now as salable as the food, so variety is the guiding principle, just as it is in the field of retail design. Restaurant design may be more demanding in some ways than other forms of commercial design, because a patron in a restaurant has much more time to look closely at the design; he also has more time to find fault with any parts of the design that are not up to par. But the goal of the designer is to combine efficient planning and layout with a design that makes the restaurant memorable; the two are necessary in equal parts to ensure the success of any restaurant.

Every aspect of the commercial interior design field has its mainstream school, and restaurants are no exception. The mainstream look of the 1970s is an extremely pleasant one—low-key, but cheerful and sophisticated. It is based on a design vocabulary that is part classic modern, part 1960s organic. Plenty of natural materials are used, but in an elegant manner. Color schemes tend to be fairly neutral as a result, with understated accents. The real beauty of this design philosophy is that it can be applied to restaurant design on any scale. It works at a fast-food operation like Arby's, but it can also be translated into a luxury setting like Les Ombrages in France, where natural materials—wood, leather, and fabric—are perfectly detailed and elegantly proportioned. Everything is kept simple, but it's also of the best quality. It can be effective in creating a cheery, chic little restaurant like Confetti Café in New York, or it can be the prototype for a whole chain of no-nonsense health food restaurants such as Healthworks. The mainstream vocabulary works equally well in a large, raw, "warehouse" space, which is what the designers of the U.S. Steakhouse started with, or in a tiny, unprepossessing space—the Sacco Caffé was transformed by judicious use of simple but striking materials. It is an approach that has been widely used, perhaps because it is so easy to knock off—it is difficult to go too far wrong when using such low-key components. But there are restaurants and there are restaurants, and the trick is to make the vocabulary look fresh every time. Interestingly enough, most of the restaurants described here are located in urban areas, which may indicate that many city dwellers are growing tired of visual overload

and prefer a calm dining environment—at least for the next few years, anyway.

Paralleling the widespread interest in architectural and historic preservation is the trend toward restaurants that are designed in adaptive reuse or renovation projects. These restaurants tend to have a nostalgic air about them, whether by accident or by design; the inherent architectural elements often have a dignity that evokes a vivid picture of the past. This design outlook is the total opposite of the "theme" restaurants that exploit the modern fad for nostalgia. You won't find gas lamps or player pianos in any of these interiors; good design from the past and the present does the talking instead, and it speaks far more eloquently than ersatz Tiffany lamps. The design can involve a building with genuine historic value, as in the sensitive remodeling and renovation of the Katonah Railroad Station, which serves as a real station by day and as a restaurant by night. It can also start with a not-so-old building that had a special character, such as the Art Deco studio building that was transformed into the airy, elegant commissary for Paramount Studios in California. In both, the design is kept simple, but the details are of high quality, creating an atmosphere of unself-conscious good taste.

Finally, there is the increasingly popular trend toward the remodeling of warehouse space; generous proportions and plenty of natural light are often the built-in advantages of these interiors. Even two walk-up apartments can be transformed into a cheery dining spot, as was the case with a restaurant called, oddly enough, The Basement. On the other hand, a warehouse with a view—of the Golden Gate Bridge—can become a sunny, calm space filled with original artwork and hand-carved furniture, as in Greens restaurant. All of these projects use extremely simple, classic modern furnishings and materials—in some cases with a rather high-tech look—in older buildings to great advantage. Their architecture is the drawing card, and the designers were all sensitive enough to support it with a subtle design scheme. Of course, the economic plus for these restaurants is that they are generally successful in helping to revive run-down neighborhoods with a relatively small investment—which certainly is easy to swallow.

No discussion of current restaurant design would be complete without some mention of the "theme" restaurant, that ephemeral concoction that so often caters to a passing public whim, only to close its doors when the fancy passes. Theme restaurants are often packaged, from interior design to menu selections,

but every now and then one appears on the scene that is truly original and humorous, as is the case with The Sandwich Construction Company. The temporary look of its naked wood frame and corrugated metal exterior, its warning signs, drop cloths, and blueprints provides a witty, lighthearted atmosphere—no one takes it too seriously, and no one is expected to. It is unpretentious and effective, and if we must have theme restaurants, they should all be so intelligently conceived.

Finally, there is the grand gesture in restaurant design. If one were to draw a parallel with a trend in the current retail design scene, this might be called "dining as theater." Essentially, this approach is based on the notion that apart from its function as a place to eat, a restaurant should be a showcase for its clientele. This philosophy allows the designer to pull out all the stops in the use of color and materials to achieve the maximum dramatic effect. Although this goal can be achieved using a modernist vocabulary, the current preference seems to be the use of period furniture and vivid color for such interiors. The historical recall can be quite literal, as in Café Fanny, which is patterned after a nineteenth-century Viennese café; or it can be eclectic, as in Le Premier, which features everything from nineteenth-century French academic paintings to Art Deco accessories, with a sensuous touch of Art Nouveau added for good measure. At One Fifth the contents of an Art Deco ocean liner transform the ground floor of a New York apartment building into one of the most romantic and urbane restaurant interiors in town. Just sitting in one of the chairs from the original S.S. *Caronia* takes you back to the days of steamer trunks and champagne parties in staterooms. A distinctly Deco mood is expressed through a 1970s vocabulary in Gordana's, a posh Chicago restaurant in which sleek brass banding punctuates an apricot and green color scheme. In projects such as these, everything is orchestrated to make the customer look wonderful. Soft lighting, warm, rich colors, dark wood, mirrors—the look is totally sybaritic, totally luxurious, but never garish. It is really more than a nostalgic yearning for yesteryear; it is recognition that back in the old days, designers really knew how to make people look good. After so many years of stark white walls and chrome, people want to look and feel good when they go out to dinner—especially when they are paying luxury prices. This approach to restaurant design, by appealing to our sensual inclination, ensures its own continued popularity.

ARBY'S

Sick of golden arches? Tired of monstrous plastic clown heads bobbing and leering at you from honky-tonk heights? Well, if that kind of place isn't your kind of place, then perhaps Arby's is. Fast food presents a desirable alternative for a great many people in this busy era, and there is no sound reason why buildings that house it should not be well designed. Stanley Tigerman and Associates ably demonstrate that this is indeed possible, and with no clowns in sight.

The Chicago franchisee of Arby's wished to develop an atypical fast-food restaurant in the heart of the city's fashionable Near North Side, opposite the venerable Water Tower, the only building in the area to survive the Great Fire of 1871. Obviously, this was hardly the site where Plasticville, U.S.A., would be appreciated by design-conscious Chicagoans. The existing structure was a 20-ft (6-m)-wide, four-story building originally housing a Chinese restaurant and sporting an ersatz Venetian facade. What took place was a major remodeling and renovation infill of this structure.

A primary concern of the clients was that a western motif be created. The architects-designers incorporated rough-sawn cedar and plants into the interior to accommodate the clients' thematic concern and, rather than replace one facade with another, treated the exterior as a means of exposing the interior. This was achieved by a flush, diaphanous glass membrane.

The transparent skin operates almost as "nonarchitecture" so as to better expose ducts, conduit, and fire-protection piping, color-coded in the primary hues. Round forced-air ducts are red, electrical lighting tracks are yellow, and fire-protection elements and piping are blue.

The bold interior colors contrast well with the warm woods, and the strong architectural manner in which the interiors are treated complements the city outside. A two-tentacled stairway, the branches of which merge at the landing, leads from the first-floor serving area to the second-level dining area.

The small-scale gridding (mullions and stucco expansion joints) optically creates an interesting scale shift on the one hand, while pragmatically solving wind loading problems and resolving curved sections on the other.

Building code requirements (concerning the separation of the top two abandoned floors with fire-resistive materials) and problems of finding steel fabricators to produce the many curved steel sections necessitated a rather long construction time, but problems such as these, when overcome, result in something such as Arby's. Clowns and lurid arches are erected far too rapidly anyway.

Exterior view (right) shows Arby's quiet facade, while other photographs show the explosive effect of bright interior colors. Bare-bulb electrical fixtures on exposed yellow conduits create a pattern sympathetic to the design. Combination plan/elevation drawings (opposite page, below right) reveal first floor space (left) and second floor space (right).

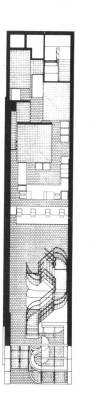

LES OMBRAGES

Rheims is the capital of France's Champagne country and the site of the great thirteenth-century cathedral that is the coronation church of the kings of France. Marc Held is a brilliant French designer of multiple talents. Annegret Beier is a likely candidate for the brightest young star of European graphic design. The extensive and highly respected Frantel hotel chain, owned by the Corestel conglomerate, has two dozen or more hotels that are all three-star or four-star.

Put these extraordinary ingredients together, and there is an extraordinary result: a 125-room four-star luxury hotel that breaks with much of hotel chains' conventional wisdom about design.

The difference in the Rheims hotel's interior is not what was spent, but how. Held realized that savings could be sensibly made by giving architect Jean Loup Roubert's basic design the respect it deserved; its structure and its reinforced concrete surfaces are, therefore, not camouflaged but exposed. This enlightened—but uncommon—attitude allowed the introduction of atypically fine detailing and atypically luxurious materials: fine woods, leathers, and wools.

The hotel's two main dining spaces—Le Duke, a mezzanine-level bar and snack bar, and Les Ombrages, a luxurious full-service restaurant—are striking spaces where concrete slabs and air ducts are covered by squares of linen stretched between parallel lighting tracks. In Le Duke, the linen squares

have the further refinement of leather fastenings at their corners. There are leather straps, as well, supporting the Hungarian-made leather cushions within the remarkable translucent dining pavilions of Les Ombrages. Detailing here is more typical of fine luggage than it is of hotel architecture.

Whereas the philosophy underlying the choice of furniture, accessories, and surfacing materials in most hotels seem to be "easily broken, easily replaced," the philosophy at the Rheims Frantel is clearly different. As in the finest of Europe's older hotels, this new one is full of fine things intended to stay in place and to age well. Held, in fact, looks forward to the day when the Frantel will no longer be considered a "new modern building" but will have taken its place quietly as an exceptionally attractive, comfortable hotel in the heart of Rheims.

(Top) Open-tread stair leads to mezzanine level; quilts add color and texture. (Right) Reception area's octagonal leather seating units are custom designed by Held. (Opposite page, top) Projecting bronze-anodized aluminum windows of the Jean Loup Roubert–designed hotel share a view of Rheim's 13-century cathedral (in background). (Opposite page, left) Detail of the key rack at the information desk. Graphic design by Annegret Beier uses the "Glaser Stencil" alphabet designed by Milton Glaser. (Opposite page, right) Exposed concrete reception desk.

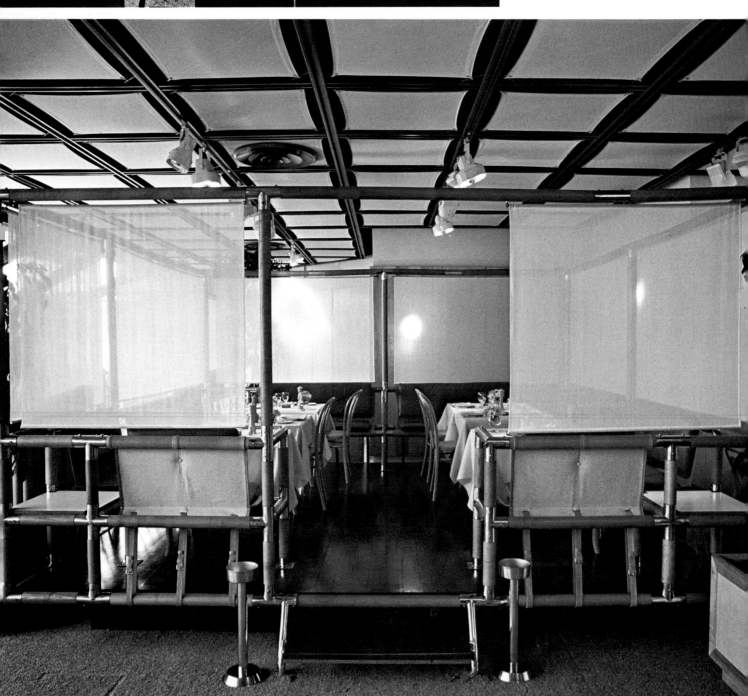

(Opposite page) Two views of Les Ombrages, the Frantel's main restaurant. Loggias of wood structure and translucent white linen panels are freestanding within the restaurant. One seats twenty, a smaller one seats only six. Ceiling squares are of the same linen, and numerous trees contribute to the "summerhouse" atmosphere. (Above) Square wood presentation buffet sits in the center of the restaurant. Two details (left) show area left of the loggia structure and linen panels.

SACCO CAFFE

Antonio Morello and Donato Savoie of Morsa Architecture and Design have built a solid reputation on the New York scene as designers who sensitively model spaces to achieve harmonious equilibrium. Their styling of the Sacco Caffé in New York City is no exception. The owner's intention was to have a small Italian-style café specializing, naturally, in espresso and pastries. And since Sacco is near a hospital, it carries a line of confectionery gift items.

As executed, the space is straightforward and honest, from its warm tile floor to its exposed ductwork. Mirror works hard in this fifty-five-seat store to expand the dimensions of the space. But it does more than that: the mirrors pick up and repeat the restaurant's major decorative and display elements to add more excitement to the space.

A lighting system of massed studio lights with barn doors is effectively directed at the restaurant's main decorative features while becoming something of a show itself. What they highlight is often carry-out stock, or humorous walls of pseudo coffee-bean sacks that add a coarse but pleasant texture to the place.

Morsa again demonstrates its skill at any scale and gives us in Sacco Caffé an example of a creative use of limited funds that puts the client's money where it will work to best advantage.

CONFETTI CAFE

New York's upper Madison Avenue at ground level is a street of galleries, boutiques, and specialty shops. Architect Ira Grandberg was challenged by the developer of Confetti Café to create a restaurant in keeping with the feeling of that neighborhood out of an old hardware store with an 8-ft (2½-m) ceiling. In this space he fashioned a seventy-five-seat restaurant that suggests four dining areas, and he did it by varying the ceiling height to break the space into zones. He was troubled with air-conditioning ductwork, but the resulting solution has a refreshing suggestion of subtle movement that makes a little space do a lot.

The restaurant does not have a great deal of window space, but room for twelve seats was found for those who wish a view of the activity on Madison Avenue. But just because they might want a view, it does not follow that they want to be one. So the designer placed a row of trees about 8 ft (2½ m) in from the window to draw the passerby's eye into the center of the restaurant.

Salmon, light green, and light cream gray blend with the restaurant's wood tones to support the appearance of a zoned seating system.

New York has a special way of making a designer work with restaurants. At Confetti Café we can see the city's way of giving ingenuity its lead.

HEALTHWORKS

Imitation may be the sincerest form of flattery in some fields, but in architecture, copying leaves the creator not at all flattered and probably financially flustered—unless, of course, the original was meant as a prototype and its subsequent reproductions or adaptations bring tangible returns. An example of this kind of provocative opportunity was the commission given to the Walker/Group to design a premier installation on New York's 57th Street for the Healthworks food-service concept.

The client's program called for the development of a standard design for a possible chain of fast health-food restaurants. The Walker/Group solution established a set of features that create a comprehensive identity for the new restaurant group.

The concept had to incorporate cafeteria service and seated and standing dining, and it had to be adaptable to a variety of space and design constraints. The prototype is a long, narrow, 3,000-sq-ft (279-m²) restaurant seating seventy-five. The site presented problems in circulation, and there is a lack of street frontage. The interior was therefore divided into three segments with a serving area in the middle. Major design elements include quarry tile flooring, ceramic tile walls, oak benches and tables, photomurals, hanging plants, exposed air ducts, and industrial lighting fixtures for an efficient and uncluttered look. Colors come from the food itself, with red and green serving as lively accents. A new logotype and a complete graphic system serve both identification and promotional functions.

The first reproduction of the original concept, on New York's 36th Street, seats fifty and has only a satellite kitchen; the bulk of the food preparation work is done in the prototype's kitchen. Optimum use of a difficult space was made by effectively organizing the bench and chair seating units. All the design elements established in the prototype are successfully applied to an unpromising site.

The next operation—in New York's Citicorp Center—was designed around an explicit set of limitations imposed by the landlord on elements such as lighting, signage, and storefront. The restaurant could maintain an identifiable image, but it had to fit into the overall character of the Citicorp Market development concept (see pages 134–137). A fifty-five-seat operation, the site has a satellite kitchen; again, major preparation work was to be done at the 57th Street restaurant.

The next major installation, in New York's Burlington House, gave the designers the opportunity to apply the Healthworks design concept to a multilevel indoor-outdoor space. The site's flexibility allowed a variety of seating arrangements approached from street, park, and building entrances. This operation seats eighty-five and includes a kitchen that took over major food preparation for the Citicorp and 36th Street branches.

An alteration to the original design solution was created for the next store, a seventy-eight-seat shop on New York's Madison Avenue. Its location in a combined residential and shopping area required that as much consideration be given to dinner as to lunch service. A variable ambience was effected with the addition of mirrors and a light-dimming system. A distinctively detailed metal storefront relates this branch to its surroundings while retaining the Healthworks image.

Boston's Quincy Market is the site for the sixth company-owned operation. This may all sound as if there is no end in sight to the project, but the Walker/Group arrangement with Healthworks is self-limiting in that it covers their mutual planning and remuneration re-

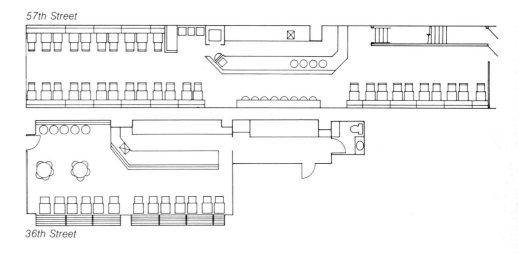

57th Street

36th Street

sponsibilities. Under their agreement, the designers developed the prototype concept and prepared basic drawings that can be used for further installations. For this they received the equivalent of a standard architectural fee. Company-owned restaurants in the metropolitan New York area are planned by the Walker/Group on a time basis. Company-owned properties outside the area are done by Healthworks's in-house architect, Bernard Reiss, with the Walker/Group monitoring construction and planning. For the first ten franchise operations—the next sites are Atlanta and Philadelphia—franchisees pay the Walker/Group a fee to get copies of the prototype plans and specifications; and the Walker/Group monitors the local architect's interpretation for design conformance.

The Healthworks design concept is refreshing in the fast-food field in that it combines natural materials and industrial fixtures to produce an environment that is both fresh and comfortable. Its high standard of design, which contrasts sharply with operations molded by less felicitous hands, will make it a good neighbor wherever it goes.

U.S. STEAKHOUSE COMPANY

Sitting down to a juicy cut of steak is nearly a sacrament of American life. What else could this extravagance be (more beef in one serving than most people in the world have in a year) but living proof of God's favor? And what could be more American than an "Old West"-style steakhouse to serve it fresh off the hoof, or perhaps an "English" chophouse? Visitors to New York's U.S. Steakhouse Company by Gwathmey-Siegel, architects, have discovered a new and notable answer, that is, a distinctly American interior that functions with vitality, intimacy, and style—an original.

U.S. Steakhouse leased half the space once occupied by the famed La Fonda del Sol restaurant, retaining the existing kitchen and the concept of a short-order food bar immediately beside the entrance for stand-up service. For the rest, Charles Gwathmey reports, "We were given a modest budget and basically a warehouse of a space." To breathe life into it, the firm divided the interior elevations into visually distinct "zones," and the floor plan into a landscape of varied seating arrangements.

Beginning at the building's existing 11-ft (3½-m) ceiling, Gwathmey-Siegel suspended downlit luminaries to a height of 7½ ft (2½ m) above the floor. This dimension is repeated twice: in the soffit of the sculptural space divider separating fast service from table service in the main dining room and in the soffit of the partially dropped ceiling over the small adjoining auxiliary dining room. From this point down a 3-ft (1-m) band of mirrors runs to a wainscot height of 4½ ft (1½ m). Both wainscotting and seating booths in natural wood rise to this same elevation from the wood plank floor.

Such a distillation of vertical space into distinct layers has the effect of obscuring the boundaries of the more than 70-by-50-ft (21-by-15-m) room. Light and form seem to glide back and forth at their own densities and velocities. The graphic treatment of the space divider, a stylized American flag, further stratifies the air around it with parallel red and white banding—a highly effective use of this almost too familiar form.

Seating is the other variable in the design

Layering of vertical space in U.S. Steakhouse offers such flux in form and scale that main dining room seems more intimate than it is. Bar and stand-up counters (above) are strong spatial elements, but graphics at concourse (opposite page, right) and soffit (opposite page, below left) play vital role in projected plan (opposite page, above left).

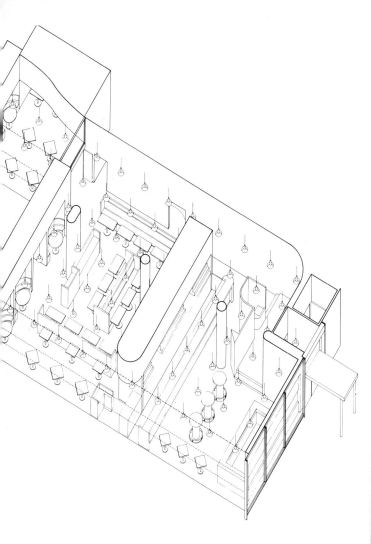

With unflagging
devotion to
Steak, Booze,
(and Old Glory)

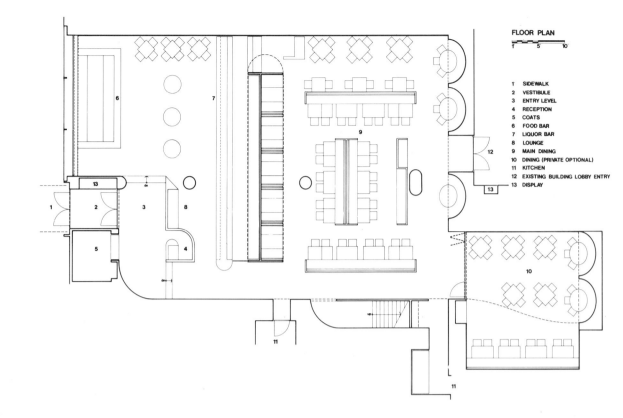

FLOOR PLAN

1 SIDEWALK
2 VESTIBULE
3 ENTRY LEVEL
4 RECEPTION
5 COATS
6 FOOD BAR
7 LIQUOR BAR
8 LOUNGE
9 MAIN DINING
10 DINING (PRIVATE OPTIONAL)
11 KITCHEN
12 EXISTING BUILDING LOBBY ENTRY
13 DISPLAY

solution, and Gwathmey-Siegel has fully exploited the possibilities with stand-up counters, bar with barstools, freestanding tables and chairs, benches with free-standing tables and chairs, banquettes, and booths high enough at 4½ ft (1½ m) that Gwathmey calls them "small rooms within the room." Visitors are given the impression that they are moving through small, intimate spaces on the broad floor; each seating configuration appears to have a density and texture of its own.

There is a dash of Americana, perhaps inevitably. Two panoramic photomurals of cattle drives at opposite ends of the restaurant define the limits of the deliberately ambiguous space. Chaste metal-framed photographs are scattered along certain walls just above wainscot height. An enlarged photograph of a cowboy and the cattle brand "U.S.S. Co." logo designed by George Lois of Lois, Holland, Callaway, graphic designers, greet passersby on the street or the interior concourse of the building housing the restaurant. Even more American is the interior design itself: lean, efficient, and resourceful. Steak could have no better garnish than this.

Use of space varies with seating configuration in Gwathmey-Siegel design. Booths and benches create room within room in main dining room (opposite page below, above, and right). Bar stools (above right) are traditional perches. See plan (opposite page, above) for overall effect.

THE KATONAH
RAILROAD STATION

In their own way, the often seedy train stations of metropolitan New York are originals with an expressive character. But as spaces to be rushed through, they command little awareness from their visitors, who ask of them only sure footing, a sound roof, and functioning mechanical systems.

Architect Myron Henry Goldfinger has taken the close-to-derelict station in Katonah, New York, and given it a dramatic rebirth as a seventy-seat restaurant called the Katonah Railroad Station. He refurbished the exterior to its original form, and he followed the same considerate course for the original moldings and wood in the structure's interior. He has resisted tampering with the past, spares us the greenhouse look, and makes a clean statement in the modern idiom with sharp angles, lines, and curves that contrast nicely with the character of the structure.

The entrance door opens into the bar, an intimate, windowless space with variable-intensity lighting. The bar is shaped like a triangle to provide maximum seating and service space. The diagonal line of the bar leads guests into the main dining room through a curved arch that reflects the existing barrel-vaulted space.

The wood in the room, all original, has been sandblasted and restored to its natural state, a complete contrast to the all-white and pure modern bar space. Hanging metal fixtures give a lower scale to the soaring space. The brown quarry tile floor is suitable for a room furnished in butcher-block tables and Breuer chairs.

The private dining room on the opposite side of the building is approached through a barrel-vaulted passage, which terminates in a mirrored wall that reflects the crisp architectural form of the bar. The curvilinear mirror extends the spatial field.

The Katonah Railroad Station is not only a restaurant; between the hours of 6:00 and 10:00 A.M. it serves its original purpose. Tables and chairs from the private dining room are removed nightly, and train passengers are left with restructured original benches for waiting-room seating, which demonstrates how a form can have two functions.

(Below) Commissary exterior is terracotta with white trim, emphasizing 1930s Art Moderne architectural forms.

(Below) Terracotta quarry tile extends to the cafeteria serving area, which has a center island wine bar.

PARAMOUNT COMMISSARY

Working on a movie lot has never been known to be trauma-free. The creative forces needed to pull off a motion picture seem to generate a highly charged atmosphere that reverberates through every corner, resulting in teary-eyed and sleepless nights for everyone from million-dollar actors to junior secretarial helpers. Any architect or designer engaged to improve a studio faces inevitable ups and down during the long haul from initial presentation to final execution. The Los Angeles office of the firm of M. Arthur Gensler Jr. and Associates, however, recently came through a year-and-a-half encounter with Paramount with flying colors.

The project—the new commissary—began as a fix-up operation, but as it went along, like all good plots, the basic theme developed with interesting complexity. Faced with a dilapi-dated space that was once the studio for "The Lucille Ball–Desi Arnaz Show," the Gensler team of Jim Clement and Phyllis Farrell was given a budget to "paint and patch." As the clients' expectations grew, Clement and Farrell soon found themselves working on a full-blown remodeling of a building destined to be the studio's "front door." Such is the competitive nature of the movie industry that the client stretched its requirements from "the best commissary in the business" to "the finest restaurant in Los Angeles." And to prove this was not just idle fantasy, Paramount hired the chef from the famous Beverly Hills restaurant Le Bistro to be in charge of the commissary kitchen!

The existing 1930s building sprawled over 15,000 sq ft (1,394 m²) and comprised two wings linked with an open courtyard. Despite

(Right) Full-service restaurant with sweeping raised floor and dropped ceiling.

(Above) Executive dining/conference room opens onto the restaurant patio.

(Above) Teal blue glass tile walls in the rest rooms reflect the graceful, curving forms in the restaurant.

(Above) Stair treads in butcher block harmonize with the golden glow of bentwood chairs and quarry tile floor.

dilapidation, some of the Art Deco character of the original structure was evident, and Clement and Farrell decided to emphasize this quality. The project called for separate facilities: a quick, serve-yourself cafeteria, a full-service restaurant, and an executive dining room for movie producers and executives. Paramount, however, was emphatic about maintaining a "democratic" attitude in respect to the different areas. For example, *anyone* can reserve a table in the full-service dining room; camera crews are just as welcome as high-echelon directors. And there are no "high-preference" tables. It was obvious, however, that the three areas needed individual definition; this was done by architectural design. The wing given over to the cafeteria (not shown) was stripped back to its original timbered trusses and has a lofty, rustic quality. The service restaurant is treated in the opposite way: a new shell with lowered ceilings and raised floor areas was inserted within the

old structure. The floors in both facilities are covered with the same quarry tile and furnished with identical butcher-block tables and bentwood chairs. (Tables are cloth-covered in the restaurant.) "Both spaces had a gymnasium quality," says Clements. "We tried to eliminate that feeling with curves, dropped ceilings, and raised terraces, which also played up the Art Moderne character of the interior."

The executive conference-dining room, which seats twelve, called for a suitable measure of luxury. This was achieved with a series of French doors and transoms, a long glass table surrounded by Brno chairs upholstered in teal blue. If all this sounds like plain sailing in interior design, the truth is rather different. Many days were spent in debating choices. Farrell recalls that the selection of details such as bud vases and salt and pepper shakers took two months.

The time and effort were certainly well spent. Paramount has an attraction that is boosting in-house morale and outside business. The company has learned the corporate wisdom of attending to peripheral work facilities. "In this industry," Clement remarks, "when everyone—writers, actors, producers, directors—earns top dollars and money is no longer an incentive, it's the perks that improve work life that count."

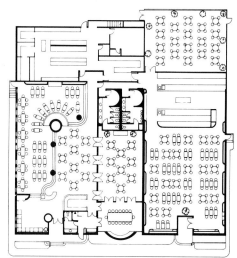

A second floor room is given a cozy, functional basementlike character with industrial lights, bar and shelving of a flexible clamp system, and pipe rail details. Even the coat rack (bottom) is built from the clamp system.

THE BASEMENT

When the two walk-up apartments above Ted May's corner saloon in Minneapolis became vacant, he jumped at the chance to develop the fifty-seat bar and restaurant he calls The Basement. Never mind that it's on the second floor and that the white ceiling frame system and lighting are reminiscent of basement pipes and fixtures; the customers are pleased with the setting and seem to appreciate the intended pun. They've kept the place hopping since it opened. Part of the credit must go to the menu of authentic Danish-style food (the owner's wife is Danish). But like credit must go to the architects, who call themselves the Architectural Framework, for providing a setting that is both refined and informal, making the chic professional from downtown and the college student (the University of Minnesota is nearby) feel equally at ease.

Entry is through a narrow recessed door at street level and up a steep flight of gray stairs, which open brightly into the center of the space. A dark blue bar and a row of bright yellow plastic globes marching down one of the white walls greet the customer. The floor is the original oak strip flooring, patched as necessary where walls were removed. The ceiling was replastered and painted enamel white with white acoustical panels spaced throughout. Two skylights over the entry stair complement the ample natural light from two adjacent walls of windows. The space is radi-

ant by day with geometrical accents of yellow, blue, and gray and light, natural-finished wood.

The long, slender 1,300-sq-ft (121-m²) restaurant, completed at roughly $53 per square foot, is visually shortened by the skillful use of the Opto clamp system of white poles and cast aluminum joints. This helps delineate subspaces within the eating area, tying it logically to the bar area. Maple bench seating along one side admittedly tends to emphasize the length, but the additional small-table seating this arrangement provides more than offsets aesthetic considerations.

Industrial lighting spaced in relation to the ceiling grid and controlled by dimmers furnishes mood lighting by night. Kitchen space and bathrooms are tucked behind the bar and were placed in such a way as to anticipate an 800-sq-ft (74½-m²) future expansion of the eating area. The construction costs therefore reflect the additional equipment investments needed for a restaurant of the intended future size.

Though the dominant white walls and ceiling betray the design's International Style origins, the use of the flexible framework, yellow steel and wood chairs, industrial fixtures, and glass shelving add strong overtones of more recent attitudes toward openly exposed technology.

The large painting on the far wall (above) is by Edward Avedisian. (Opposite page, above) Blunk sculpture forms tables and seats. (Opposite page, below) Across the Blunk sculpture looking toward the restaurant.

GREENS

An uninspiring, disused concrete warehouse may seem hardly the right ambience for dining, but with enterprise and imagination, anything can be made to work. This particular warehouse certainly had an advantage: windows overlooking a boat dock and a view to San Francisco's Golden Gate Bridge—when the famous San Francisco fog does not sweep a white cloak over it.

Tassajara means a lot to people in California who like good food. The Tassajara bakery in San Francisco is jammed all day long with

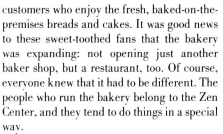

customers who enjoy the fresh, baked-on-the-premises breads and cakes. It was good news to these sweet-toothed fans that the bakery was expanding: not opening just another baker shop, but a restaurant, too. Of course, everyone knew that it had to be different. The people who run the bakery belong to the Zen Center, and they tend to do things in a special way.

The Zen group let artists take over the interior design. Edward Avedisian, who painted up a storm in the interior of the Tassajara bakery and its companion needlework shop (red, blue, and yellow walls), was assigned the job of creating large abstract paintings to hang like murals. He got so enthusiastic that he started painting equally vivid fabrics for tablecloths and banquette seat covers. Sculptor J. B. Blunk produced an amazing and vast environmental piece in carved wood that forms seating and tables at the "café" end of the restaurant. Three huge ethereal paintings by artist Willard Dixon were given a special place on a wall overlooking the Blunk masterwork. With crisp white paint and industrial roof trussing, now painted black with canister downlights punched in its rigid geometry, the restaurant has the feel of an art studio. It is the absolute antithesis of that restaurant type known as "motel modern." There is not a plastic surface to be seen, not a smidgen of heavily draped curtain, and above all, none of the gloom that so often envelopes the restaurant-goer with an impending sense of doom. Here, all is airy and light. You can actually see out. What's more, with well-placed tables and carpet to muffle sound, this is a pleasant and peaceful spot to be.

Greens, as the restaurant is called, has the visitor's welfare truly at heart. The food comes mostly from the Tassajara farm—fresh vegetables, greens, and fruit. As its name implies, the menu is strictly vegetarian. But still, you can gorge away on the desserts; and oh, those cakes!

THE SANDWICH CONSTRUCTION COMPANY

The Sandwich Construction Company in Charlotte, North Carolina, is sophisticated, yet humorous. The structure, an old Lum's, has been stripped of its signature elements and clad in galvanized, corrugated, and sheet steel siding and hand-stained diagonal pine that suggests an older look. The arrangement of these materials suggests a cluster of add-on shed-warehouse structures.

The interior has exposed ductwork, pipes, and conduit beneath a wood truss roof. The ceiling in the new entry drops down to obscure the dining area. The panorama of a half-finished multilevel dining area is revealed while patrons walk to a table. Intimate rooms or corners formed from 2-by-4-in. (5-by-10-cm) stud partitions covered by 2-by-12-in. (2½-by-31-cm) pine planking or Sheetrock in varying stages of completion divide the space.

Tabletops are 2-by-4-in. (5-by-10-cm) studs. Seating is wooden folding chairs custom-splattered by the designers. Color is introduced into the vaulted ceiling area in the form of white and colored canvas drop cloths splattered extensively with the paints used in the interior.

Notable throughout is the treatment of graphics, which were designed by Gary Hixson. Stencils provide detail for walls, rafters, and decorative elements such as the fire buckets and pails suspended from the rafters. Identity for areas such as rest rooms is treated with humor.

The restaurant's designers, Hans Fassen, George L. Beck, and Lindsay Daniel, received a first honorable mention in the Commercial Division in the 1978 Hexter Awards for this installation, which represents a complete blending of interior and graphic design.

CAFE FANNY

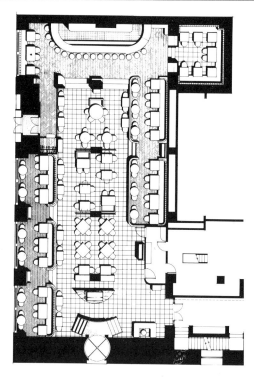

The Men's Bar at the 43rd Street and Madison Avenue corner of New York's Biltmore Hotel was never, legally speaking, a landmark interior. Psychologically, however, it was a landmark interior within a landmark building adjacent to a monument—Grand Central Terminal—that has become a battle standard for historic preservation. One does not tamper lightly with such an interior. But the Men's Bar attracted too small a segment of the public for too few hours of the day and too few days of the week. Male chauvinism had turned unprofitable as well as impolitic.

The challenge for Victor Palmieri, owner of Realty Hotels, Inc., which manages the Biltmore Hotel, was to attract more patrons for longer hours every day without turning off the old patrons who remember the old bar's dark mahogany paneling, massive oval mahogany bar, and air of solid comfort. When he posed that challenge to restaurant consultant George Lang, Lang reasoned that only another exercise in nostalgia would work and proposed a nineteenth-century Vienna coffeehouse.

As planning proceeded, Lang proposed to name the establishment Café Fanny, after the legendary Austrian ballerina Fanny Elssler, and devised a bill of fare that includes six varieties of schnitzel, Viennese tortes, strudels, and other confections, a choice of coffee *mit oder ohne schlag*, and Austrian wines and spirits. And music—Mozart, Strauss, and the like on the tactful sound system by day, and a live violin and piano duo at dinner.

Daroff Design Inc. has done nothing to jar memories of the old Men's Bar. Nothing looks too new, slick, or pretentious. All is solid: dark mahogany, marble, brass, and plush. Yet Daroff has completely transformed the interior architecture and circulation with a two-level floor plan in which a higher, ban-

quette-framed rim area encloses a lower central floor. Aisles are wide, service stations are conveniently placed, circulation is clearly defined, and the stair structure is gracefully curved. Over the lower core area the ceiling appears coffered; wood moldings frame raised ceiling panels that happen to be acoustical tiles.

Additional space was annexed from an adjacent former boutique. More space was captured for new niches along the wall through the redesign of the heating and cooling system. The variety of seating arrangements—in chairs, settees, and banquettes—provides "special" places for all to see and be seen along the excellent two-level sight lines. A row of new Madison Avenue windows advertises the presence of the café, though low lace curtains on brass rods shield guests seated at window tables.

Daylight from the windows varies the lighting over the hours of operation. Even at night the café has a warm and elegant sparkle the old bar never had—from the glow through the deep rose taffeta lampshades, from the mirrors that cover much of the small private dining room and relieve the dark surfaces of the big main-room mahogany columns. Mahogany-framed glass dividers near the Madison Avenue entrance not only shield diners from wind as the door is opened, but add their share of warmth and sparkle through starbursts, bevels, and other cut decorations on the glass.

Necessary changes precluded the use of the existing mahogany paneling, which was carefully disassembled and stored. The big oval bar was given a matching back bar but was moved to the rear. The new *pièce de résistance* near the cashier's station is the brass and mahogany *pâtisserie* from which you choose pastry. It is a replica of one made more

CAFE FANNY

than a century ago and still in use in Vienna.

Custom millwork went into the tabletops—some of Red Roncivalous–Breche Nouvelle marble, some of solid African mahogany. A venerable grandfather clock from the Biltmore's lobby is only one of many antiques, along with some of the service stations and much of the brass hardware and fixturing. Fixtures not antique, including the alabaster chandeliers, were designed by the Daroff firm, as were the wood and brass newspaper racks near the cashier's station and in the small rear private room.

Noticeable objects and surfaces are expensive; inconspicuous ones took the budget squeeze. For the easy maintenance essential to long, continuous hours of use, the lush cocoa velvet on the banquette backs—channel-tufted and contrast-welted—is matched with vinyl for seat cushions. It is only the outsides of the wood-framed setees that are up-

holstered in authentic Josef Hoffmann brocade. The insides, again, are vinyl. Solid mahogany tabletops are polyurethane-treated to resist staining. Chairs and barstools in high-traffic areas are simply detailed, sturdy stained beechwood. Lower-level floors, checkerboard-paved in creamy white Italian and black Belgian marble, require only mopping and a bit of buffing, as does the upper-level herringbone wood parquet.

It remains to be said that the windows have been given an arch with a gold-edged field of black paint overhead, and that the cocoa and cream graphics and facade graphics, awning, and doors strike exactly the perfect balance between Viennese flourish and contemporary sophistication. The night we dined there incognito, some Austrians at a neighboring table, who had obviously been there before, looked right at home.

A treasury of French Art Deco pieces is joined by contemporary accessories and materials under the skillful supervision of architect Sam Lopata to create Le Premier restaurant. Note finely detailed ceiling, whose five shifting planes give form and direction to entire room, etched glass panels (opposite page, left) antique bar (opposite page, right middle), and original Art Deco pendant lights in upstairs banquet room (opposite page, right below).

LE PREMIER

Flick your fingernail beneath Le Premier's glossy skin, and wondrous images come forth: a neighborhood bistro set within a hall of mirrors, men and women in formal evening attire promenading in a warehouse, nineteenth-century French academic paintings looking suspiciously good amid sleek Art Deco architecture. This paradoxical synthesis is Le Premier, a new French restaurant and social club in New York City, designed by architect Sam Lopata. If the imagery seems outrageous, the planning and installation do not. The restaurant, set in a two-story turn-of-the-century brownstone, runs as smoothly as a *Cordon Bleu* kitchen.

That it should is no accident. Lopata, who arrived here not long ago from Paris, shares a

deep respect for the culinary arts with the owners, one of whom is a former chef himself. "First come the kitchen and services," says Lopata. Given the disposition of the building's two upper stories and basement, he placed the main kitchen on the ground level, a service kitchen above, and a preparation kitchen, wine cellar, and storage below.

Planning the main kitchen came next. "I simulated a ship's galley," Lopata explains. "Without space to place cooks around four sides of the standard open stove, I lined units up." In other words, meat, fish, and other specialities move in a line up to the executive chef, who puts final touches on each dish before sending it out. The remaining food preparation facilities received the same studious

concern: room to work, ample storage, stainless steel equipment, white tiled walls, and tiled floors. "This kitchen's a real beauty," says Lopata with pride.

Le Premier's ground-floor dining room with bar, private social club on the upper floor, and rest rooms in the basement took shape in a most unorthodox way. Lopata and the owners acquired most of its accessories in Paris before the formal interior design was ready. How could this be? "I had already prepared basic layouts for these spaces," Lopata points out. "And we knew we wanted to incorporate French Art Deco motifs in a modern design. Since I don't like to plan what I cannot fulfill, we took off for Paris."

What the group shipped back was a small treasure trove of artistic masterpieces: tables, lighting fixtures, a carved wood bar, lace curtains, painting in the "Art Pompier" nineteenth-century academic style which is enjoying renewed critical and popular interest, and even a magnificent stained-glass window two stories high. Lopata augmented this with compatible local materials and furnishings; where nothing commercially available filled his needs, he designed his own solutions. (Lopata has to his credit several modern furniture pieces that have been sold through American retailers for years.)

Inspiration to assemble these fragments into an interior design came literally in the night. "I awoke with the idea of creating a five-tiered ceiling," Lopata recalls. "The use of stepped-back planes put everything else into order. The design came soon after, and then a model that the clients loved at first sight."

The carved wood bar commands the middle of the ground-floor dining room, but it is the boldly conceived gallery perspective that draws guests inside. At the core of its logic are the ceiling and floor, those traditionally neglected planes that Lopata has treated as dynamic Cubist compositions. Their overlapping expanses of form and color (the floor's various wood grains follow the ceiling lines) create an almost palpable force field to which all other design elements in the room pay homage. If it all seems like a mirage, it is one filled with highly original details: graceful brass trim on salmon-colored walls and ceilings, lush suede-covered chairs and banquettes designed by Lopata in twenties pro-

files, delicate lace curtains silhouetted against exposed brick walls, cove lighting hidden in the ceiling's many folds, shimmering backlighted etched glass panels celebrating the charms of extravagant ladies in period costumes, those "Art Pompier" paintings, and exuberant bouquets of silk flowers.

Passage to the private social club upstairs is by way of a kaleidoscopic staircase of brass railings, dark green carpet, mirrors, and the Art Deco stained-glass window, all of which replace a freight elevator Lopata had removed. Upstairs is divided into a backgammon room, staircase foyer, and banquet room with service kitchen. The mural covering the foyer's walls, whose women frolicking in a sylvan setting stop just short of being florid, sets the proper ambience for the club. To the front, the backgammon room offers gaming tables, comfortable chairs, and soft lighting surrounded by dark green channeled upholstery walls with brass trim. To the back, the banquet room extends the layered ceiling, lace curtain, and wood floor theme with handsome period pendant lights and steel shelving.

Downstairs at Le Premier contains more surprises. For one thing, Lopata plays off the upholstered wall treatment he used in the backgammon room against a wine cellar of exposed brick and glass to conjure the sense of a subterranean "window." Then, the ceiling is coffered to suggest higher elevations. As a final flourish, highly upholstered restroom interiors are accented with broad mirrored surfaces.

Lopata, who also acted as general contractor (as he does for virtually every project he designs), feels he has designed a contemporary interior with Art Deco variations, and not vice versa. Surely such deliberate contrasts as exposed brick against etched glass and lace, and "Art Pompier" against Art Deco, are manifestations of a more independent way of thinking. Were there any rules at all for Lopata to follow in creating Le Premier? "The kitchen must work," he says, "and the restaurant should be a showcase, where everyone sees everyone else in the most beautiful setting possible." Good company, good food, and good surroundings: for our schizophrenic society, this must be heaven.

Ladies at leisure in staircase foyer mural by William Riggs (above) set style for adjoining rooms of social club at Le Premier. Staircase itself (far left) is kaleidoscope of brass railings, stained glass, and mirrors. Wine cellar (left) enhances basement with some of the glories of France.

ONE FIFTH

Its floors don't sway beneath you. There's no salt spray in the air. But New York's One Fifth restaurant, by artist-designer Kiki Kogelnik, is the lighthearted reincarnation of a cruise ship. In the summer of 1974 the *Caribia*, christened Cunard's S.S. *Caronia* in 1948, sank en route to the scrap heap during a typhoon. Fortunately, the ship had already been gutted and her Art Deco fixtures sold to appreciative collectors such as Ms. Kogelnik and her husband, Dr. George Schwarz. What was evidently the soul of the vessel is now the heart of an unusually coherent and successful interior design.

Kogelnik combined those fragments from the ship with such skill that it is easy to believe they were intended for One Fifth Avenue itself, an Art Deco apartment building. Her guiding principles: an artist's sense of composition, a commitment to quality, and sheer perseverance—to design and build One Fifth in just three and a half months.

The two dining rooms and U-shaped bar wrapped around a spacious steel kitchen are a painterly exercise of light, color, and texture. The design draws people from the street into a small, bright, simply described dining room with clam bar, piano platform, and period painting by Winold Reiss. It pulls them through a long, dark passageway lined with wood, mirrors, and warm glowing lights and releases them within a large, soft-textured, intimately lighted dining room complete with portals framing twelve sepia prints of an ocean wave by photographer Ernst Haas. Every fixture relates closely to everything else in terms of scale, spacing, and alignment to create the sensation of one grand orchestrated movement.

If some of the fixtures are not those of the ship, the majority are still authentic to the period. Why this fascination with Art Deco? "It is attractive in its own right," Kogelnik says, "the last great decorative style of this century. It is also the environment I grew up in."

And the ship? "One Fifth is where you can leave New York behind, at least during the meal." Among the many diners who seem to agree are former passengers of the *Caronia*, who often identify themselves by bringing memorabilia along, now that their "ship" is in port again.

On board One Fifth: main dining room (opposite page) looks onto historic Washington Mews, whose low elevations permit sunlight to flood the interior by day; other views of room (top left and right) show dessert cart and window treatment using Ernst Haas photograph in different croppings, flanked by sconces and topped with cove lights. Smaller dining room (above left) is simply detailed setting for Winold Reiss painting, visible at rear. Bar (above right) connects two dining rooms in dark, romantically lighted passageway that draws guests through U-shaped floor plan.

GORDANA'S

It must be like walking into a nicely wrapped box of colored marzipans and what a way to begin a meal. This is the comfortable atmosphere at Gordana's, a posh new Chicago restaurant designed by Zakaspace, the firm headed by Spiros Zakas.

Situated on the fourth floor of a brand new building, the restaurant does a brisk trade, despite a slightly awkward location. One arrives via elevator and is then deposited within a realm of apricot and hunter green. Though color and fabric choice play an important role, they are still merely the icing on a well-designed, well-organized cake. Walls in the bar and the first dining area are dark mahogany, relieved by horizontal bands of gleaming brass. A second dining area, one which will eventually serve as an entrance to a future garden, has walls of bolstered hunter green suede padding. These too run horizontally, thereby contributing to the overall restful quality. An illusion of floating is achieved by lights beneath the carpeted risers. One can pretend to be on an extended European cruise, languidly sailing through the Mediterranean.

Green banquettes lining the wall are divided by glass panels in window-pane form, reflected by identically treated wall mirrors. The effect this produces to the eye is one of openness, while functionally it serves the ear, affording acoustic privacy.

The main dining room has dark gray walls, offset by furniture upholstered in deep apricot, and houses a number of sedate, yet pleasantly surprising custom touches. Floor-to-ceiling venetian blinds are custom built of mahogany slats, and velvet apricot padding surrounds mirrors decorated with a sandblasted strip and the G logo. Another Zakas custom touch is the superbly fashioned calla lily wall sconces. The success of these touches is due entirely to their "unforced" spirit. Obviously, the same care that was taken in creating them was taken in selecting them.

Carpeting is of elephant gray, interspersed with a tiny, irregular chocolate-drop pattern ("as if someone spilled M&Ms," says Zakas), and is relieved by a border of solid gray. The ceiling is sectioned into four stepped-down layers, each harboring recessed lighting.

Wandering musicians, with violin and guitar, float through the spaces, a pianist performs in the main dining room, and the Chicago press has given rave reviews to the food as well as the design. It is evident that this gift-wrapped candy box is quite a successful lure.

SHOWROOMS

The question "What is a showroom?" is one of the hottest issues in today's commercial design world. In one respect, showroom design is especially meaningful to designers, since the people who ultimately use these spaces are other designers—whether they be architects, interior designers, product designers, or fashion designers—who can be especially critical and demanding. Starting with the premise that a showroom is a place in which goods of one kind or another are displayed for a nonretail market, the design approach taken can depend on any number of variables, all of which, of course, are ultimately rooted in marketing. The client—that is, the manufacturer—wants his merchandise to be displayed in the most effective, straightforward, and flattering way possible. But even given those requirements, there is a great deal of room for invention and innovation. And although showrooms have for many years been a field for experimentation by some of our most talented architects and designers, in the past few years this spirit has experienced remarkable growth. The eclecticism that has recently characterized architecture and interior design has been a boon to the showroom field, since it has also promoted a fresh approach to merchandising. And although these spaces are essentially geared to professionals, there seems to be plenty of room for show business—even the pros like to be amused and entertained.

In terms of a design philosophy, showroom designers seem, these days, to fall into one of two camps. The first and more traditional outlook is based on the theory that in a showroom, the merchandise—furniture, fabrics, carpets, or whatever—is the focus of attention, and therefore the architecture or interior design should play a secondary role. The design should certainly be able to stand on its own merits, but it should ultimately be unobtrusive, the better to be supportive of the goods on display. This philosophy can take any number of forms, but the general mode is one of classic modernism, since its design vocabulary—flat surfaces, simple elements, and lack of decoration—provide a neutral backdrop. That does not mean, however, that such design cannot be lighthearted. In the case of the Knoll showroom in Houston, white and blue "sails" frame a vaulted ceiling—a playful touch in an otherwise low-key setting for the display of furnishings and fabrics that are classic examples of modernist design. The interiors, carefully modulated in spatial terms, are not allowed to interfere with one's appreciation of the goods; instead, they support it by creating a psychologically pleasant environment using elegant proportions and details.

The modern vocabulary can also be expressed in a very carefree manner, as in the case of the MIRA-X showroom in New York. A small, cheery, multilevel space is kept as neutral as possible, the better to show off the company's coordinated lines of fabric and carpet. The "total design" concept of the firm is illustrated through the grouping of colors, patterns, and textures in related materials. Its approach is effective.

Reflecting the broader trend toward no-frills design is the Professional Kitchen showroom in New York, a restaurant supply house. This is a place where serious cooks come to look for equipment, as well as a place where designers search for kitchen and restaurant furnishings. Therefore, it is only appropriate that the place has a no-nonsense look. The materials are of a type that has become known as high-tech: rubber flooring, track lights, steel posts and shelving, with walls painted a severe but rather elegant gray. In fact, the design is the merchandise itself—perhaps the best advertisement of all. The overall message here is professionalism: if you want the best tools of the trade, here they are, and no fussing around. This design and others like it are based on the idea that the best way to display merchandise to professionals is without embellishment.

In the case of the Brickel showroom in the Pacific Design Center in Los Angeles, however, the pared-down look is presented in a more luxurious manner, befitting the style of its contents, which happen to be top-of-the-line furniture and fabrics for contract and residential application. The entire design is based on a single geometric theme and is carried out with elegant simplicity and rigorous attention to detail. The architectural scheme provides total support for the merchandise on display, unobtrusively but impeccably. These qualities also characterize the Andrew Geller showroom in New York, where women's shoes are displayed in an underplayed but perfectly proportioned and beautifully finished space. It is small but jewellike, with details such as handmade cabinetwork and an island of granite set into the carpet—the "little things" that often mark the best of classic modernist architecture. Materials are simple but luxurious; they are, of course, deliberately subdued so as not to detract from the merchandise on display. This attitude toward showroom design is one that is always fresh and new, no matter how many times it is seen. Some may call it the "safe" route, but it is, in many cases, the most pleasing. Even within the boundaries of its aesthetic program there is always room for variation, as in the Steelcase showroom in Chicago, where a clean white two-story space is dramatized by a striking spiral staircase, a marvel of form and

exquisite detail, not to mention engineering.

A final example of the merchandise-as-display approach can be found in the Eurotex showroom in Philadelphia, in which one could actually say that the merchandise becomes the showroom itself, with the client company's carpet covering walls, columns, and steps—an unusual but effective method of getting the merchandising point across.

The other current in the stream of showroom design today is the "showroom-as-display" philosophy, which holds with the theory that suggesting a stage set can effectively exploit the temporary nature of showroom display to the best advantage. Fantasy, historical allusion, and unorthodox use of colors and materials are all ingredients in designs of this type, derived in many respects from the principles of retail design. The trick is to make showroom spaces inviting and entertaining, to create a more dramatic setting for display. Merchandise is often incorporated into the design in a theatrical manner, as in the Sunar showroom in New York, where a Tuscan pergola has been re-created for the display of the company's fabric collection, which is draped from white latticework and hangs against terra-cotta pink columns. This is hardly understatement at work, but neither is it overstatement; it makes its point by appealing to our subconscious, our sense of history and playfulness. And there is an added element of fun in the fact that the display is temporary, a stage set to be knocked down and replaced by yet another. The use of historical allusion also characterizes the Erbun Fabrics showroom in New York, in which a tiny space is transformed by the addition of lattice-covered walls that were inspired by the work of Scottish architect Charles Rennie Mackintosh.

The all-out glamour approach is typified by the Pace showroom in Miami, in which a skylit atrium, dramatic lighting, angular walls, and other luxurious touches create a feeling of fantasy chic. The setting is the perfect sort of presentation for the glamorous merchandise.

Finally, a combination of modern architectural elegance and subtle historical references characterizes the Thonet showroom in New York. This design seems to combine the best of both philosophies in a spectacular and exhilarating showroom environment. High-tech materials are used in definitively non-tech, soft colors, with low-key details accenting the dramatic architectural space. The furniture is readily visible at all times and seems most appropriate to its rather fantastic setting. A perfect balance has been achieved between the setting and the product. This is the ongoing problem in showroom design, and the seemingly endless variations of its solution are what makes it so fascinating.

KNOLL INTERNATIONAL

Take a very ordinary space—3133 Buffalo Speedway in Houston to be exact—give it to Sally Walsh, partner in charge of design for Houston's S.I. Morris Associates, architects, to fill with Knoll furniture, and what do you get? A Knoll International showroom: calm, classic, and unexpectedly breezy. For above one long and narrow space is a vaulted ceiling framed with white and blue (an old Knoll trademark) "sails" masking a balcony.

The former staff member of Knoll Associates designed the Houston showroom to be a simple but elegant foil for furniture in the Knoll tradition. Furniture is organized into groups suggesting reasonably sized room settings, "so that an individual can more readily relate the scale to the space he will be furnishing." Carpet is everywhere, reflecting the widespread use of carpet in the facilities of Knoll clients. A neutral color scheme permits clients to "spread samples of fabric in myriad colors, to select combinations without distraction." Bright color is restricted to the textile display.

What inspired this breath of fresh air? According to the designer, one notable inspiration was Knoll itself. "Knoll has long been famous for its willing production of standard items in special materials and finishes," she says. "We have succumbed to that temptation in a few of our selections. But we have also found joy in traditional Knoll understatement. The incredibly fine collection of good designs in furniture and textiles made this project for Knoll a most pleasurable experience." (It shows.)

In other words, the design is a return to Hans Knoll's basic idea: "élan with simplicity." The modulation of space, the studied application of color, form, and texture, and that soaring vaulted basilica are accomplishments of a most original designer.

MIRA-X

In New York the entire MIRA-X collection of textiles and floor coverings is all together for the first time in the arrestingly redesigned balconied and terraced townhouse at 246 East 58th Street that Fabrications recently outgrew and that once housed an antiques dealer. Now, retail traffic flows through the first floor and mezzanine of the retail store—Coordination—which also stocks accessories made from MIRA-X fabrics (including stuffed toys), table accessories, and china.

The two floors above the store are trade showrooms where fabrics used as hangings are displayed on roller bolts, or shown as upholstery on Strassle of Switzerland furniture. Architect for the building's interior remodeling was Hans-Uri Schweri of Switzerland, where MIRA-X is based.

Danish-born Verner Panton, noted architect and designer, created the MIRA-X concept. In brief, it provides "total living harmony" from a palette of fifty colors, from the naturals to variations of brightness, that harmonize by twos or by dozens for fabrics, rugs, and carpeting. Fabrics range from cottons, linens, and wools to hand-printed velvets, stretch knits, and others woven with metallic threads. Six geometric patterns are produced in three repeat sizes to allow specific effects for different spatial proportions. Carpeting, varied in style and fiber, includes handmade Berbers.

Cascading fabrics, a pillow "tree," and stuffed toys on the balcony (right) demonstrate compatibility of the fifty colors of Verner Panton MIRA-X program.

PROFESSIONAL KITCHEN

Harry Friedman loaded a pushcart with crockery in 1889 and worked his way through Manhattan's Lower East Side to found a restaurant supply house that still bears his name. Today, H. Friedman & Sons is a major supplier of food-service equipment and table service, with engineering and design services for architects, interior designers, and restaurateurs, to customers across the nation and around the world.

In the Professional Kitchen, H. Friedman has gathered some of the finest kitchen service equipment available today for restaurant, hotel, institutional, and residential use in a showroom designed by architect Burt Stern that is as much a joy to behold as the products are. The secret of its success is simple: the products are the interior design. Gray walls, black rubber flooring, track lights, and jewellike steel shelves and racks make ample room for a brilliant display of copper, aluminum, and steel pots, pans, ovens, and other implements that can satisfy even the most fastidious hotel chef.

"Our products are built to last," says Harry Stern, vice-president. "Architects and interior designers, who often seek our advice, will find a wide range of equipment meeting heavy-duty institutional needs as well as those of the serious cook."

Everywhere at 18 Cooper Square (across the street from fabled Cooper Union) the emphasis is on quality. Should architects and interior designers need guidance, there is a fully qualified technical staff. Designers should also think of their own personal kitchens; according to Stern, "It's not unusual for them to end up buying for themselves, too."

The showrooms of Brickel Associates Inc./ Ward Bennett Designs in Space 260 of the Pacific Design Center (8687 Melrose Avenue in Los Angeles) are a reminder of Ward Bennett's accomplishments as a total designer. Everything in this 2,400 sq-ft (223-m²) space is unified by one thematic form—a long cylinder with radius corners—which happens to be the geometry of Bennett's Capsule Desk Group. By encapsulating the showroom's storage and office space behind a curved wall in the rear, he used this shape for the main space of the showroom and for the raised display platform he built between two columns. The thematic form is reinforced by the light cove filled with spotlights and by the seamless black rubber base stripping. It also appears as the glazed opening in the polished steel floor-to-ceiling door, and even in such details as the polished steel electric sockets.

In contrast with most mart showrooms, which are glazed for maximum visibility, Bennett's 45 ft (13½ m) of corridor walls are masked with 12-ft (3½-m)-high panels of polished steel. But curiosity can be satisfied by moving up close to the four round bulls-eye windows. The come-on is irresistible. In the interior is mostly white space with natural cocoa matting on the floor and plenty of potted trees.

The associated Los Angeles design firm is Timothy H. Walker & Associates, with Ted Teshima as senior designer.

Main showroom space (above) centers on open floor area, with granite panels set flush with carpet for shoe modeling. Wall panels at end of room rotate for shoe display (opposite page, above). Similar materials and details are seen in an auxiliary showroom (above right). Reception area (right) features silk tapestry designed by Breuer.

ANDREW GELLER

Throughout his distinguished career, Marcel Breuer's work has employed contrasts of materials that are sometimes surprising and always felicitous. In his early houses there were frequent juxtapositions of light wood framing and rugged fieldstone, or of concrete fireplaces standing before walls of glass. In this recent showroom-office for the Andrew Geller shoe company, there is another such surprise: a little island of honed-finish charcoal granite set flush (actually, set *very* slightly lower to preclude stepping against the edge) with the surrounding wool carpet—a practical and almost irresistible spot for twirling about in new shoe designs. Here and throughout the office and showroom areas, colors and materials are luxurious but hushed; nothing is allowed to upstage the shoes. The reception area, however, is brightened by a Breuer-designed tapestry, executed in 100 percent silk. Cabinetwork detailing is impeccable, as is expected from the Breuer firm. Herbert Backhard was the firm's partner in charge; Jane Yu was the interior designer.

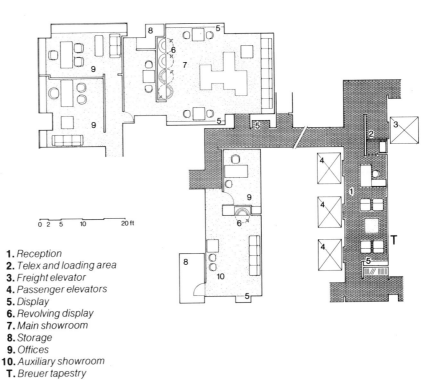

0 2 5 10   20 ft

1. *Reception*
2. *Telex and loading area*
3. *Freight elevator*
4. *Passenger elevators*
5. *Display*
6. *Revolving display*
7. *Main showroom*
8. *Storage*
9. *Offices*
10. *Auxiliary showroom*
T. *Breuer tapestry*

STEELCASE

Neocon XI's most eagerly awaited unveiling in 1979 was that of the layered Steelcase showroom, doubled in area by the acquisition of a tenth-floor space directly under and exactly the duplicate of the firm's eleventh-floor space in the Chicago Merchandise Mart. The 1970 redesign of the eleventh-floor space had been a milestone for the firm. With it, Warren Platner conveyed the message that Steelcase was on the move before Steelcase had products to support it. He made the space *itself*—a crystalline white space where individual pieces were showcased like works of art—the talk of the design community. A stroboscopic photomural and over 7 tons of clear glass in the suspended ceiling were among its talked-about features. So was its cost.

The design of the tenth floor and of the staircase between floors was taken on by Harry Weese of Chicago. His job was far

more complex and stringent than Platner's: to make the floor "a stage for changing events in systems furniture development," that is, to present settings rather than single pieces.

Weese has selflessly subjugated his ego, obtaining the necessary visual compartmentalization not on the floor but on the ceiling, where coffers have been built with low thresholds, leaving the floor a natural wood stage. After Platner's dazzle, Weese's seems a shadowy environment. Were it otherwise, no one would observe the displayed systems, particularly the task/ambient Lite-Savers.

Only sharp observation reveals how superbly and unobtrusively Weese has solved planning and engineering problems here—massing reverse pyramid column clusters to buttress the heavy floor, from which the staircase opening had removed an essential column. Particularly neat is Weese's way of fitting air vents and electrical supply lines for the track lights in reveals that accent the ceiling and columns like a linear motif.

After all the publicity about the staircase that Weese designed to lure people between floors, it is surprising to step on it and dis-

cover that it is totally firm underfoot despite its visual transparency. It is a spiral, fanning outward like a seashell as it drops, of laminated wood treads (Weese wisely decided to leave the natural wood grain showing) without risers or posts. What holds it firm are tensioned stainless steel rods 5/16 in. (8 mm) in diameter—strings of steel.

The meticulous engineering of the staircase, however impressive, is less striking than its beauty. This is the result of its transparency. Never has steel proved a more attractive complement to wood.

EUROTEX

Designers of the super showroom for Eurotex, in Philadelphia's Marketplace decorative furnishings center, have created an environment where the products do not engulf one, but are applied through design as sculpture. The 1,700-sq-ft (158-m²) ground-floor space is wrapped in the Berber and Tretford carpets and Acousticord wall coverings for which Eurotex is famous.

Earth-tone textures flow up and down steps, around walls and concrete columns, enveloping bleacher-type benches, encasing the horseshoe-shaped reception desk and furniture bases. The building's 16-ft (5-m) ceiling height allowed splitting the space into two 7½-ft (2½-m) levels. Bright colors of carpets and rugs are integrated with the architecture, recessed into walls fitted with swing racks. Time-saving "help-yourself" samples are tucked into wall cubicles. Area rugs and handmade wall hangings provide decorative accents. High-beam track lighting supplies drama throughout.

The showroom was designed by Douglas Kahn of Gordon-Kahn Associates, a New York architecture firm. Stephanie Mallis was the interior designer. It was planned, says Mr. Kahn, as a fun place to be in—and that it is.

THE PACE COLLECTION

The Pace Collection's striking showroom at 47 N.E. 36th Street in Miami, designed by Pace design staff's Denise Marchand and Janet Schwietzer, is an aesthetic achievement with a twist. Attractive settings have been provided for Pace furnishings in a two-story, 10,000-sq-ft (929½-m²) structure centered around a skylit atrium. Less obvious is that this handsome facility replaces a "flophouse" hotel in a once blighted section of town. Pace completely gutted and reconstructed its building. It also paid to redecorate adjoining buildings and to plant native flora.

Yet the building demands attention. Art Deco exterior details have been cleaned and simplified to create a forceful facade. Inside, light pours through the triangular skylight, to which angular walls, carpeted and lighted platform steps, lush plants, and a glazed entrance (whose tile runs out to the sidewalk) respond sympathetically. There's even a touch of legerdemain. To find the elevator to that seductive second-floor balcony, you must first pass through tempting Pace displays. If this be a "trick," there are "treats" as well: the Pace Collection and its next-door neighbor, David Harrison's popular restaurant Food Among the Flowers. Food for body and soul—what more could one ask?

SUNAR

Subliminally, as you stroll through the new Sunar showroom, you are promenading through an allée of massive architectural columns tinged terra-cotta by the sun's glow. Psychologically this is a garden idyll, a timeless mythic scene of classic grape arbors and latticed pergolas. Only instead of grapes, sheer fabrics hang from the lattices, and heavier-textured wools and velvets are loosely looped into the grids. Carefully aimed lights dramatize the transparency of the sheers and the delectable surfaces of the upholsteries. It is impossible not to handle them.

What a glorious way to display glorious fabrics! And when you consider that the massive architectural columns are nothing but lightweight, inexpensive cardboard forms for concrete, circled at the base by wooden halfrounds, this evocative stage setting becomes more glorious still. The entire allée can be moved or rearranged easily—instantaneously—and the effective adjustable lighting snaps onto the grid. Weeks after the illustrated presentation of the Sunar International Textile Collection at the Sunar showroom at 150 East 58th Street in New York, the col-

umns were moved to a smaller room to make way for a furniture display. Sunar showrooms in Los Angeles, Houston, and Chicago use the same system.

All of which goes to prove that Sunar president Bobby Cadwallader has lost none of his acumen as a talent scout. Who else would have had the courage to hire Princeton University architecture professor Michael Graves—winner of a Prix de Rome and a National AIA Award, and standard bearer of the intellectual "Five" postmodernists—to design a system of showrooms to launch a new enterprise in a blaze of glory and high sales? But then who else would have gotten a team like Sunar Textile vice-presidents Barbara Rodes-Segerer and Duncan South to produce so original and superb a fabric collection from scratch (manufactured in Scotland, Ireland, Germany, the Netherlands, Denmark, and the United States) in less than a year? We already know Douglas Ball's "Race" system for open offices, but can hardly wait for the furniture by the Vignellis, Niels Diffrient, Richard Sapper, Don Pettit, Warren Platner, and Gianfranco Frattini.

Architect Michael Graves (right) stands in one of his instant grape arbors flanked by a fall of Christa Haeussler's "Transline" and Anni Albers' "Maze." (Below) Other cloth displays.

ERBUN FABRICS

The concept of an indoor street is the idea behind this immaculate showroom designed by architect Robert A.M. Stern. The streetscape is created with mirror inserted into a grid of articulated latticework, and the end result has a distinctly Georgian flavor—not surprising when you remember Stern is a champion of the British nineteenth-century architect Lutyens, although, he adds, "Mackintosh was in my mind here; there are no curves, the grid is flat and abstract." With a bluestone floor and stools for seating, the showroom is clean and elegant without being minimal and offers no

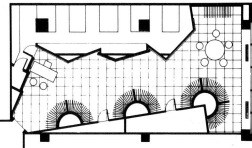

competition to the fabrics, arranged in three drumlike carousels opposite the lattice "windows." This is as it should be, of course. "People must be able to look, see, find samples. But they must be aware of an aura that makes them want to return."

Hints of Palladio, a "medieval street," and the Temple of Luxor nudging modern minimalist details suggest that John Saladino has been at work. Stepping out of the elevator at the Decorative Arts Center in New York into the Thonet showroom brings you into a curiously bare space, enclosed by a half-round unpainted plaster wall, or nymphaeum, which defines entry in the architectural vocabulary of ancient Rome. Five bolts of cloth, looking like minimal art, lie casually on the white tiled floor. Their colors—terra-cotta, beige, celadon, gray, and aubergine—signal a visual Morse code to the discerning eye. These are Saladino's colors. They will be Thonet's colors for upholstery in the 1980s. The then-and-now character of the showroom entry plays on another dimension relating to corporate image: Thonet's 150th anniversary.

The graceful, quiet elegance of the Romanesque entry leads to a platform with a shattering panorama ahead: the 59th Street bridge against the Manhattan skyline, exploding and expanding in mirrored panels at either end of a long stretch of slanted windows; Saladino likes to draw on such juxtapositions in his interior design work.

The showroom unfolds on three levels, in a chaotic order that registers Saladino's talent for creating a modern space within a framework of historical references. Thonet's furniture is divided into three distinct sections, color-keyed on "rivers" of carpet in celadon, gray, and aubergine, basking beneath a celadon-painted "sky" overhead.

Saladino's orchestration of materials—plaster, tile, and carpet—is augmented by the silver plastic laminate used for counters and tables. "I like this material because of its ambiguity," he says. "You can't tell what it is. It could be lacquered wood or stainless steel. It requires you to look before you find its message." For Thonet, the total landscape is dynamic, a celebration of the past that leaps ahead to the twenty-first century.

(Opposite page, above) Triple-level showroom with celadon-painted ceiling descends from a white tiled area beside the window into a softly carpeted space. (Opposite page, below) Skylight windows have mirror panels at each end to expand the Manhattan skyline view and flood the interior with natural light.

MALLS & MARKETPLACES

The 1960s saw the appearance of a new phrase in our vocabulary: *shopping mall*. A far cry from the suburban "shopping centers" of the previous decade, these generally enclosed clusters of retail shops and stores, ranging in size from small to vast, have become a standard part of the American retailing scene. The idea behind the shopping mall is that placing a wide variety of stores under one roof, so to speak, provides greater convenience to the shopper and, even more important for the retailer, increases a store's exposure (and therefore potential sales) simply by virtue of its proximity to the other stores. Instead of driving from one place to another, the suburban mall patron can take a leisurely stroll through whole groups of shops. When he gets tired of shopping, he can stop at one of several restaurants or fast-food stands that are part of the mall scene. Sometimes he can even see a movie; many of the larger malls have at least one theater. It is an artificial environment created for the convenience and comfort of the consumer, as well as for the ultimate profit of the retailer (not to mention the developer of the project). During the past few years, the mall has become sufficiently established as a building type to allow for a good deal of variation in conception and design, in order to suit the geographic, demographic, and marketing requirements at hand.

For purposes of classification, it can now be said that the shopping mall comes in two varieties: urban and suburban. But the classic shopping mall of vast proportions is a peculiarly suburban phenomenon, because of the ready supply of land in those areas and because of the market that exists for a great variety of shops housed in one spot—a market created by the automobile. This is the type of development that proliferated throughout suburban America during the seventies. The Hulen Mall in Fort Worth is a classic of this type. With its open space-frame grid and its skylit roof, it is a climate-controlled "shopping street." Its generous use of trees and plants, and water in the form of a reflecting pool and fountains, makes it an example of the best type of mall design—a gardenlike, neutral, but inviting setting for a variety of retail operations from mammoth department stores to tiny boutiques. The very neutrality of the mall design takes its cue from a real street, which is relatively unadorned save for natural light and trees, receiving its liveliness

from the diversity of stores that line it, as well as the groups of people who shop there. With the addition of restaurants and the pushcarts that dot the space, the mall takes on the atmosphere of a bazaar, and it becomes a place to socialize as well as to shop. The point is to make sure that people have such a good time that they will return again and again.

The Hulen Mall is certainly representative of the mainstream approach to mall design, but new and different types of suburban shopping malls have been appearing recently. Some of them are small in scale and specialized in appeal, but the basic concept is the same: to bring a sense of the bazaar to the suburban shopping experience. One of the most interesting examples of the "new mall" is Mayfair in the Grove, in Florida. Mayfair is unusual because of its emphasis on architectural decoration and handicrafts. Hand-carved woodwork, ceramic tile, stained glass, copper etching, and relief sculpture are all part of its design program, as is energy efficiency: it is cooled and ventilated naturally, which is a sharp departure from the hermetically sealed controlled climate that is typical of many shopping malls. Mayfair is also unusual in that it caters to a particularly affluent market, shoppers who are just as appreciative of quality in architectural design as in product design. The diversity of the consumer market, happily for us all, supports this and other variations on specific building types, so that innovative projects like Mayfair in the Grove can exist and flourish.

The shopping mall concept has proven successful in urban areas as well, but on a rather different scale. In fact, it might be preferable to call these urban shopping clusters "marketplaces" instead of malls to differentiate them from their suburban counterparts. For one thing, the relative scarcity of land and floor space in large cities precludes the vast layouts typical of the suburban shopping mall; instead, urban marketplaces tend to be designed on a smaller scale. For another, urban geography and demography are such that an urban mall could not support the great variety of stores found in the suburban mall—those stores already exist in urban neighborhoods, so there is no added convenience in placing them together in an urban marketplace. These mini bazaars rather tend to emphasize what seems to be a special passion of city dwellers: food. Whether in the form of restau-

rants, takeout stands, or specialty food shops, large cities seem to be able to support an almost endless variety and number of retail establishments that are devoted to eating. For this reason, food seems to be the biggest drawing card in the urban mall setting. And an extra bonus of this food consciousness is that the existence of small cafés and food stands encourages people to congregate and stay awhile, thereby creating a lively atmosphere and a sense of warmth that personify the best spirit of city living.

A now classic example of the urban marketplace is The Market at Citicorp Center in New York. In terms of design, it is something of a suburban shopping mall turned on end; it occupies the bottom three floors of one of the city's most spectacular skyscrapers, and its sun-filled atrium is a constantly crowded gathering spot for New Yorkers who stop at its food stores or restaurants. The Market also fulfills an important urban-planning need: its restaurants replaced the small neighborhood restaurants that were displaced several years ago by the construction of the office tower.

Another example of an urban marketplace that is given over to food shops and restaurants is the World Trade Center's concourse-level market. The lobby is edged by food-service facilities that serve people who work in the building as well as those in the neighborhood. Several degrees of formality are offered, from a stand-up coffee-and-croissant breakfast to an elegant dinner in a softly lit restaurant. Clean, functional, but warm decor characterizes these spaces; in marketplace settings such as this, the most popular ambience is a sort of snappy efficiency—but one that is far from cold. The use of natural woods, plants, ceramic tile, and bold graphics has a broad-based appeal, possibly because many of these materials are so closely associated with cooking and kitchens in people's minds—a positive association, because it makes people hungry.

But ultimately, the goal is the same for urban and suburban malls and marketplaces: to create an atmosphere of liveliness, diversity, and above all novelty. The American shopper seems to be a particularly insatiable consumer, ever hungry for new forms of entertainment, and it has become the role of the modern-day bazaar to provide that entertainment.

HULEN MALL

While the country of Fort Worth, Texas, has experienced a steady population growth each year, the southwest has expanded faster than other sections. In 1978 permits were issued for some 1,000 new homes in the immediate area of Hulen Mall, which was built shortly after another nearby shopping center opened—both off Loop 820.

In the evening Hulen Mall sheds a welcoming glow from its skylight and clerestory roof, an open-frame space grid of trusses mixing glass and clear shatterproof acrylic to create a climate-controlled "shopping street" that hints of a botanical garden or the late, lamented Les Halles in Paris. It's a people place, humming with activity. It's a shopping center, a flea market, a picnic ground, and a civic center all in one, where the expressed desire of architect and client to "make shopping fun" has been accomplished.

Hulen Mall, designed by Hellmuth, Obata + Kassabaum, is in true Texas dimensions—200,000 sq ft (18,587½ m²) on two levels, each 530 ft (160½ m) in length, with the lower-level mall open to the upper level. At either end of the glass-roofed mall are two full-line department stores: Sanger Harris and Montgomery Ward. Between the stores there is a mixture of more than eighty merchants operating specialty shops that sell everything from shoes to chemises, as well as boutiques where one-of-a-kind vintage collectables and handicrafts can be found.

Restaurants in the mall are either oriented toward an outdoor fountain in a reflecting pool, or turned indoors toward the profusion of plants and flowers. Merchandise and florists' wares are rolled out daily to the "street" on pushcarts, contributing to the effect of an international sidewalk bazaar.

The mall is also utilized for community events, through its performing and exhibition areas, and has a community room that seats 100 persons.

HOK's client, and the developer of the mall, was the Rouse Company of Columbia, Maryland, a farsighted firm famous for its highly successful community developments and a multitude of malls, one being Quincy Market in Boston. Those most involved with Hulen Mall from the Rouse Company were John Boorn, development director; Laurin B.

Askew, Jr., director of design; and Ken Walter, director of construction.

HOK first prepared a design criteria manual which encouraged "bold, thoughtful design of individual stores while ensuring an orderly, yet lively, character for the mall as a whole." The manual included design criteria for storefronts and display windows, lighting, and signs. HOK's graphics department was responsible for all graphics. Charles P. Reay, of HOK's St. Louis office, designed the awnings, which function as a secure enclosure when the stores are closed.

Commitment by client and design professionals alike was that a pleasant, stimulating environment would influence people to linger in the mall, put them in a happier frame of mind, and encourage repeated return visits. The more attractive the aesthetics of the design, the more effective the commercial success of the project.

To this end the design philosophy followed certain forms to implement the functions. To create an indoor shopping street, pavers, trees and tree grates, pools, fountains, and street furniture were specified. Slender steel structural columns extend from the first floor to the open steel roof trusses, interfering minimally with the light and airy effect. Warm, neutral colors, grading from off-white to warm grays, were chosen for structural members to avoid conflict with the colors used in storefronts and their awnings. Special graphic effects, the shopping carts, casual table and chair arrangements, and an antique steeple clock point the public to areas of special interest. The specially designed decorative lighting clusters on the entry canopies and columns, also an HOK design, add their sparkle to the festive environment that draws crowds to Hulen Mall in the evening. Besides being a convenient place to shop, Fort Worth residents find it a needed facility to act as a showcase for their talents and activities.

Steel trusses, skylights, and clerestories combine with exposed ducts to add excitement to the mall. For security, red canvas awnings lower to cover shop facades at closing time. Awnings and custom light clusters are both HOK designs.

Section

1 Open Mall
2 Garden Court
3 Fountain Court

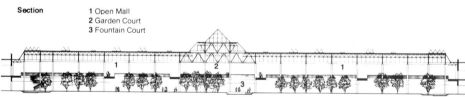

Second Level

1 Offices
2 Tenant Space
3 Open Mall
4 Garden Court
5 Fountain

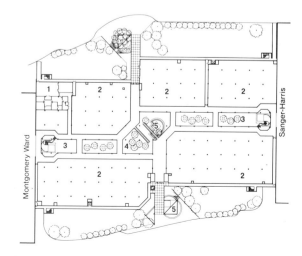

MAYFAIR IN THE GROVE

(Below) Motorized skylight; (bottom) courtyard gazebo; (right) escalator atrium.

"If I had my way," says architect Kenneth Treister, "no one should have to go to a special place to see art. It should be all around." With this dictum in mind, Treister, who has been pursuing a radical direction in architecture for the last thirty years, seeks to blend art and crafts into architecture to a degree that few have thought of doing before. The Mayfair in the Grove shopping complex represents his philosophy in a most developed sense. Here is a three-story emporium of shops where every surface is decorated with some form of handicraft—woodwork, stained glass, tile, copper etchings, wrought iron, and concrete relief. For the first-time visitor, it's an astonishing and dazzling conglomeration

that goes far beyond notions of theatrical lighting, graphics, and color in producing a shopping experience that is "entertainment." This is a real rival to the ethnic bazaar because it maintains a sense of personal touch throughout.

Inspiration for much of the ornamentation came from Treister's constant travels through the Caribbean and Central and South America, where he absorbed Mayan and other ancient cultural embellishments. What is significant is that it is all integrated here into a concrete structure that is inherently twentieth-century and includes current technology—such as a motorized sliding skylight over the escalator banks which automatically

protects shoppers in unfavorable weather. Treister delights in a constant "then-and-now" juxtaposition of concepts in a design. The location of the complex is Coconut Grove, Florida, which experiences a year-round tropical climate, but the public spaces in the building have *no* air conditioning. Treister structured the building to include the centuries-old concept of wind tunnels for cooling purposes. There are two large central courtyards, with narrow breezeways leading into them. As the sun draws hot air up and out of the courtyards, cooler air is drawn through the passageways to fill the vacuum. In 90° weather, you can stand in those cool passageways and feel the breeze swirl around you.

"People said I could never put up a successful shopping complex, particularly a really high-class one like this, in Florida, without air conditioning," Treister laughs. "But I have proved them wrong." The natural air conditioning produces a comfortably pleasant environment in which to stroll from shop to shop. The enticement to linger is all around: there is a canopied gazebo to sit in, pools and fountains to reflect on, balconies to lean over and from which to observe the scene, benches to rest on. Shopping at Mayfair in the Grove can easily be a day-long experience with more than forty top-echelon shops to visit, from Charles Jourdan to Pierre Balmain and Valentino, with the Ginger Man, the Magic Pan,

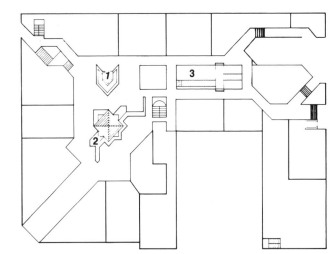

1 Elevator
2 Ornamental gazebo
3 Escalator atrium

and two other restaurants offering varied refreshments and relaxing banquettes for rest in between.

The unfolding of excitement and novelty from floor to floor, around corner to corner, is similar to the spontaneity and unpredictability of an ethnic market. A key element in creating this sense of random choice for shopping is the varied access. A glass elevator cage rises through one of the courtyards, its copper doors hammered with symbolic motifs done by artist Roy Butler. Brass-railed escalators crisscross the other courtyard. They rise from a plaza of fountains that play onto a surface of tiles, cracked into thousands of frag-

ments and laid in kaleidoscopic, geometric arrangements of colors. The third method of access is stairways, given handsome ornamentation with elaborate wrought-iron railings.

Treister set the stage and the standard for the shops in the Mayfair in the Grove, and part of the success of the enterprise rests on his control of aesthetics. He has encouraged all tenants to be extraordinarily inventive, to continue the extravaganza experiences in the terra-cotta-brick walkways and public plazas outside their stores. (Those who do not are gently informed that their ideas and operations are best transferred to another milieu.)

The Julio unisex hair salon by Dennis Abbé (see pages 56-57) is probably Treister's favorite example of interior decoration, with the Pierre Balmain men's shop running a close second. Treister directed the architectural design of the Balmain shop himself, choosing rare Chinese antiques as counterpoints to modern lighting and display racks. He is proud of details, such as stained-glass screens and hand-crafted woodwork for accessories. "As a sculptor and artist myself, I appreciate the smallest piece of handwork."

When it comes to decorating the concrete forms of his work, Treister creates the initial design himself, working alongside artists he

employs in his Florida studio. Intricate molds are branded in Styrofoam and applied to forms of the structure before the concrete is poured, producing organic, integral ornamentation.

Treister's work has been compared to Frank Lloyd Wright's for its respect of nature. On one side of Mayfair, balconies are shaped to accommodate great oak trees, and the sidewalk below undulates to accommodate their roots. "People also say my work is Mayan, or Pre-Columbian—they use a lot of different words to describe it," he says with a grin. Of course, in the end, it's undeniably Treister.

Tucked under the tall legs of Citicorp's sleek tower are the angular granite-faced form of St. Peter's Church (at right in photo above) and the stepped-back element (right), containing the atrium-centered shopping mall. Tucked inside the tower, interiors full of innovations. The tower's rakish roof (opposite page) gives Manhattan a new silhouette; curtain wall mirrors the sky and neighboring buildings.

CITICORP CENTER

The construction of architect Hugh Stubbins's $128-million Citicorp Center in New York was the subject of continual controversy from the announcement of its plans until its completion. Questions arose about every aspect of the three-building complex, which includes a fifty-nine-story office tower, a separate seven-story building with a central atrium and three-story shopping mall, and the new St. Peter's Lutheran Church. Those questions can now be answered: St. Peter's Church is functioning as one of the most successful urban churches in America. The structural and electrical innovations that make Citicorp the most energy-conserving building in the world are all working perfectly. The shopping mall is one of the most exciting spaces in New York. The Citicorp tower on its 127-ft (38½-m)-high piers, placed midface on each of the building's sides, visually opens up an entire city block. The tower is not only not awkward, but, coupled with the ease with which the space of each building flows into the next, it has provided a superb model for future urban planning. Citicorp Center is a resounding success.

The most obvious starting point in any discussion of Citicorp Center is its 914-ft (277-m) tower. Capped by a 160-ft (48½-m), rakishly sloping crown, Citicorp is the seventh-tallest building in New York City and the tallest bank building in the world. The sloping crown was designed for aesthetic reasons; only later was a solar energy collector considered and ultimately rejected. Citicorp uses 60 percent less energy than any other building of comparable size in the world *without* solar collection, thanks to the energy-saving systems built into Stubbins's original plans.

The three-story shopping mall, simply called The Market, is perhaps the biggest success of the complex. The first announcement of The Market, built around the theme of food and its preparation, met with considerable skepticism. The only indoor mall of such scope ever to have worked in New York is the concourse level of Rockefeller Center, whose success is largely based upon the facts that it is a much used link between Fifth and Sixth Avenues and that it provides access to a crowded subway station. But Michael Buckley, president of Halcyon Marketing, Inc., whose idea The Market was, used the successful elements of Rockefeller Center and researched the needs and buying habits of New Yorkers to come up with an idea that seemed bound to work in the dramatic skylit atrium created by Stubbins.

There is nothing, however, so convincing as fact. Now, even though the novelty has faded, finding an empty table in the large central area on the atrium floor or on the balcony above it is often quite difficult. New Yorkers even more than tourists are enjoying this unique area.

The concept works because it does, in fact, meet a real need. Many of the buildings torn down to make way for Citicorp housed restaurants of various types, at varying price levels. The Citicorp Market has replaced them with French, Hungarian, Greek, Swiss, and various other restaurants, as well as a *pâtisserie*, *boulangerie*, smoke shop, and bookstore (with a large cookbook section). You can buy anything there from the ingredients for a meal to the meal itself. And you can either eat in a restaurant or bring food out to one of the tables in the atrium. There are several inexpensive restaurants in the center, but none is a fast-food place. The level of the food quality matches the variety and the ambience. The shop that probably attracts the most attention, however, is Conran's, the English-based home furnishings chain (see pages 22–27).

Like Rockefeller Center, Citicorp's Market is a link between two major avenues. It is also adjacent to the main access to one of the busiest subway stations in New York, which empties into the complex's sunken plaza and directs traffic up to the street or into the tower lobby. As one enters the lobby, at subway or street level, the atrium and bustling Market are visible immediately ahead.

The atrium carries the materials of the exterior of the complex into the interior. Thus the terra-cotta bricks of the plaza and sidewalks are the flooring of the low-rise element, and the walls between floors of the atrium are the same natural-finish aluminum as the building's skin. The continuation of exterior materials indoors is not uncommon, but it is especially impressive at Citicorp, where it aids in integrating structures of such diverse function. Each unit of the complex maintains its own identity, but the integration of the structures as part of a larger entity is as complex on the inside as it is on the outside.

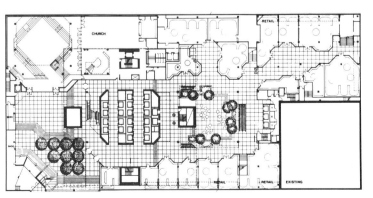

"The Market," though bustling with shoppers and diners, centers on a restful oasis of trees and seating designed by Sasaki Associates (opposite page) that has become one of New York's most popular midtown spots. (Above and left) Some of the restaurants and food-oriented shops surrounding the atrium.

Largest of the World Trade Center's new concourse-level restaurants is a self-service facility called The Big Kitchen (general view, above; detail, left). Checkerboards of colored tile are a motif repeated throughout. Custom seating recalls the cane upholstery of turn-of-the-century streetcars. (Opposite page) giant letters (by graphic designer Milton Glaser) announce the restaurant boldly, while serving as space dividers and even occasional seating.

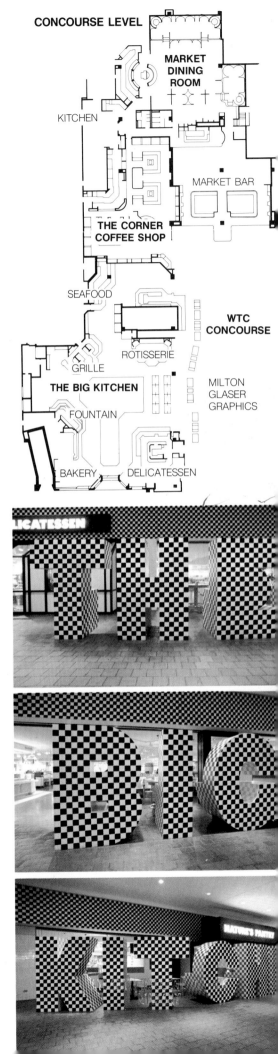

MARKET
DINING
ROOM

KITCHEN

MARKET BAR

THE CORNER
COFFEE SHOP

SEAFOOD

WTC
CONCOURSE

ROTISSERIE

GRILLE

MILTON
GLASER
GRAPHICS

THE BIG KITCHEN

FOUNTAIN

BAKERY   DELICATESSEN

WORLD TRADE CENTER

Cole Porter imagined being "Down in the Depths on the Ninetieth Floor" many years ago, and when the twin towers of New York's World Trade Center (WTC) were finished, some architecture critics felt that such elevated depression had become a reality. But things perked up considerably when, at the very top of 107 floors of aluminum banality, Warren Platner designed a strikingly effective observation deck; when Platner's Windows on the World restaurant opened atop the *other* 107-floor tower, things looked even brighter. Now there is also cause for celebration at the base of the towers.

Under the plaza that connects the towers and is ringed by smaller buildings of the complex, there is a major concourse-level lobby connecting the buildings above, the streets around it, and the intricate tangle of subway lines below. Serving a working population of approximately 80,000 tenants and about 150,000 additional visitors daily, this is undoubtedly one of the busiest lobbies on earth. It also happens to be on the site of the historic Washington Market, where the best edible merchandise in New York has sold. How natural, then, for the lobby to be edged by food-service facilities, and how lucky for all those hungry thousands that the facilities have been so cleverly planned and admirably executed!

The planning began when the Port Authority (owners of the WTC complex) hired Joseph Baum as its food-service consultant. Baum, formerly of Restaurant Associates, may be more responsible for good restaurant design in this country than any other single person—without ever having designed a single restaurant. For it was Baum (along with Jerry Brody, president of Restaurant Associates) who was asked by Philip Johnson to collaborate with him on the Four Seasons. It was Baum who then continued the radical idea of working with first-rate designers by asking Alexander Girard to do La Fonda del Sol. He has continued the policy in collaborations with William Pahlmann, Warren Platner, and others over the years.

For the WTC, it was Baum's concept to recapture some of the character of the Washington Market, with its bustling street life, its variety, its tempting displays of fresh vegetables, spices, hot muffins, meats, and fowl. He visualized this market spirit interpreted in a variety of food-service situations, some self-service, some with waiters, and all linked to a single food preparation center. The Port Authority liked Baum's ideas: Inhilco, a division of Hilton International, was brought in as operator of the restaurant group; and Inhilco, in turn, hired Baum to implement his own ideas. James Lamantia of New Orleans was commissioned as architect for the concourse-level restaurants, and the firm of Harper & George was chosen as interior designers.

The result is bright, unpretentious, and appetizing. Two floors below the concourse level, there is a single giant receiving and food preparation center, some of its facilities (the bakery, for example) also serving the glamorous Windows on the World high above. On the concourse level, there is a surprising variety of dining choices.

Largest of these, with 500 seats and places at stand-up tables, is The Big Kitchen, a fast-food operation (according to design critic Paul Goldberger of the *New York Times*, "far and away the best-designed fast-food restaurant in New York City"), but it is by no means a large, impersonal cafeteria. Food service is divided among many different counters, each with its own specialty: raw clams and oysters, for example, or delicatessen sandwiches, health foods, ice cream, or grilled meats. Someone could, in fact, eat in The Big Kitchen every day of the week and never have the same sort of food or stand in the same line twice. In the morning, several of the counters are converted for service of coffee, tea, hot croissants, and other breakfast specialties that may either be eaten at the tables or taken to offices; after lunch, some counters are converted again for the sale of take-home goods: breads, cakes, or complete meals.

Because most of the food preparation is done in the commissary two floors below (and therefore away from the restaurant's high-rent location), there is virtually no back-of-the-house space on the concourse level. Final food preparation there (slicing the cheese, dressing the salad, opening the clams) is done by the same employee who serves the customer and in the customer's clear view.

A smaller, adjacent facility is The Corner Restaurant, an attractive area with waiter service at counters or at small tables. A free-standing kiosk nearby, The Coffee Exchange, serves coffee in the mornings, and a choice of hot soups (with bread, fruit, and wine) at lunch; also available are packaged teas and coffees to take out, and even a selection of handsome teapots and coffee makers. In an-

other section are such curiosities as food-based medicines and cosmetics: herbal teas, rosewater, avocado hand cream.

Throughout these facilities, checkerboards of white and colored tiles (or white and colored squares of plastic laminate) are a constant unifying motif. Even the servers' uniforms match. The biggest checkerboards of all are to be found on enormous three-dimensional "trees" and on letters (spelling out THE BIG KITCHEN) that are big enough to sit on or even to snuggle up in with a sandwich and a beer. These oversize graphics, serving simultaneously as sign and space divider, are by Milton Glaser.

There is also a quite elegant restaurant area called The Market Bar & Dining Rooms. Here the lighting level is considerably lower, mixed drinks are served, and both the menu and the decor are more elaborate. But not overly elaborate: Harper & George has managed the small miracle of creating a Victorian atmosphere without fuss or plush, and an unmistakably sophisticated dining room without tablecloths (on some tables) and even without carpet. Natural woods and pumpkin walls and ceiling prevail, sparked with handsome lighting fixtures and etched glass space dividers. Even here there is generous variety: in addition to the main dining room, there is a grille room (with drinks and elaborate hamburger meals), a bar with food service, and a 150-seat café, a perfect spot for people watching at the edge of the concourse lobby.

The total achievement: dining facilities for 1,100 that have extraordinary life, personality, efficiency, variety, and charm.

(Opposite page) Four of the many food counters which serve The Big Kitchen. (Above) A grille for hot meats: an under-counter exhaust system makes an overhead hood unnecessary. (Below) A marble-countered delicatessen department, a take-home bread shop, and the Seafood Market & Raw Bar. White tiles with checkered emphases, brass highlights, and natural woods are the primary materials; servers' uniforms, sympathetically, are crisp white with checkered aprons.

(Above) A counter of checkered plastic laminate separates a cafe area from the WTC's concourse-level lobby. The Corner Restaurant is at the left; the Market Bar and Dining Rooms in the background. (Opposite page, left) Milton Glaser's whimsical topiary near the entrance to Nature's Pantry, a health-food section of The Big Kitchen. (Opposite page, right) A freestanding kiosk called The Coffee Exchange offers breakfast items in the morning, hot soups at lunchtime. (Above right) A vaguely Scandinavian look characterizes The Corner, a 150-seat facility with waitress service at counters. (Middle right) The grille area of the Market Dining Rooms, woodsy, dark, rather masculine, with heavy brass details. (Right) The main dining room of The Market: the air of a fine restaurant, but strikingly spare and clean. The stepped ceiling planes in pumpkin color add visual interest and deflect sound.

ILLUSTRATION CREDITS

Ardiles-Arce, Jaime, 18–21, 82–85, 120–123
Baitz, Otto, 74–75
Baldwin, Byron, 90–91
Cabanban, Orlando, 16–17
Citibank, 134
Crane, Tom, 92
Cserna, George, 136–137, 138–143
Daniel, Gibson, 91 (exterior)
Davidson, Darwin, 115
Dirand, Jacques, 68–71
Fine, Elliot, 28–29
Freiwald, Joshua, 42–43
Georges, Alexandre, 93–95
Giovanni, Raeanne, 22–25
Kivett, Paul S., Architectural Fotografics, 38–41
Kolleogy, Fran, 14–15
Lefcourt, Victoria, 74–75
Lilley, Weaver, 44–49, 114
McGrath, Norman, 76–79, 80–81, 135
Miller, Melabee, 30–33
Naar, Jon, 26–27, 56–57, 88–89, 116–117, 118–119, 130–133
Obata, Kiku, 126–129
Perron, Robert, 34–37, 96–99
Rand, Marvin, 8–9, 10–13
Raycraft, James, 50–51
Rooks, Marius, 112–113
Rosen, Laura, 110–111
Ross, Mark, 54–55, 100–101
Schell, Catherine, 52–53
Staller, Jan, 72–73
Turner, Philip, 66–67
Vicai, James, 62–64
Warshol, Paul, 108
West, Stu, 86–87
Wynne, Dan, 22–25
Zakas, Peter, 102–103

INDEX OF DESIGNERS

Abbé, Dennis, 56–57
Architectural Framework, 86–87
M. Arthur Gensler Jr. and Associates, 82–85
Askew, Laurin B., Jr. (Rouse Company), 126–129
Avedisian, Edward, 88–89
Backhard, Herbert (Marcel Breuer), 110–111
Bahat, Ari, 54–55
Beck, George L., 90–91
Bennett, Ward, 109
Bier, Max (Bier, Boxt and Hirsch), 28–29
Blackman, Andrew, 22–25
Blaine, Alice, 34–35
Blunk, J. B., 88–89
Boorn, John (Rouse Company), 126–129
Bottineau, Jean, 50–51
Bromley, Scott, 18–21
Conran Associates Ltd., 22–25, 26–27
Copeland, Novak & Isreal, 8–9, 10–13
Daniel, Lindsay, 90–91
Daroff Design, Inc., 92–95
Environmental Planning & Research, Inc., 42–43
Fassen, Hans, 90–91
Goldfinger, Myron Henry, 80–81
Grandberg, Ira, 73
Graves, Michael, 116–117
Greene, Martin, 36
Gwathmey-Siegel, 16–17, 76–79
Harper & George, 38–41, 138–143
Held, Marc, 68–71
Hellmuth, Obata + Kassabaum, 126–129
Hollein, Hans, 58–61
Hugh Stubbins and Associates, 134–137
Jacobsen, Robin, 18–21
Kahn, Douglas (Gordon-Kahn Associates), 114
Kogelnik, Kiki, 100–101
Lamantia, James, 138–143
Lois, George (Lois, Holland, Callaway), 76–79
Lopata, Sam, 96–99
Mallis, Stephanie, 114
Marchand, Denise (The Pace Collection), 115
Morello, Antonia (Morsa Architecture and Design), 73
Polito, Bill, 37
Pomodoro, Carmelo, 36
Robert P. Gersin Associates, 30–33
Saladino, John, 120–123
Sartogo, Piero (Sartogo Architects and Associates), 62–64
Savoie, Donato (Morsa Architecture and Design), 73
Schweri, Hans-Uri, 107
Schwietzer, Janet, 115
Secon, Edward, 46–49
Stanley Tigerman and Associates, 52–53, 66–67
Stedila Design, Inc., 14–15
Stern, Burt, 108
Stern, Robert A. M., 118–119
Stull Associates Inc., 50–51
Teshima, Ted (Timothy H. Walker & Associates), 109
Treistler, Kenneth, 130–133
Walker/Group, 74–75
Walsh, Sally (S. I. Morris Associates), 106
Walter, Ken (Rouse Company), 126–129
Weese, Harry, 112–113
Welton Becket and Associates, 10–13
Yu, Jane, 110–111
Zakas, Spiros (Zakaspace), 102–103